PRAISE

"With equal servings of humor and candor, Alexis Paige opens a window to her writing life and demystifies the idea that writers live in a fairytale world of ongoing success and creative contentment. Instead, she leads us through the often uncertain, sometimes treacherous, deeply vulnerable, and always messy, territory that maps the land in which most writers live. Part memoir, part craft guide, her book inspires us to explore and make mistakes, to set attainable goals, to ask for help, and to savor the rewards that inevitably surface when we keep returning to the chair. I feel like I've been given the gift of companionship that I didn't even know I was looking for."

MELANIE BROOKS, AUTHOR OF *WRITING HARD STORIES: CELEBRATED MEMOIRISTS WHO SHAPED ART FROM TRAUMA*

"With her accustomed wit and insight, Alexis Paige has written a memoir that is also a craft book, a guide to leading a writing life for those of us whose days are messier and more hectic than most books of writing advice allow for. I recommend this book to any writer whose life isn't spent in a cabin by a lake, or a room of their own, but out doing the complicated work of being a person in this world."

SARAH EINSTEIN, AUTHOR OF *MOT: A MEMOIR*, THE ASSOCIATION OF WRITERS & WRITING PROGRAMS AWARD FOR CREATIVE NONFICTION

"Alexis Paige shows us how a subtle shift in perspective will sometimes reveal that the writer's life we yearn for and the writer's life we live are actually one and the same. Thoughtful, instructive, profoundly useful—not to mention spit-out-your-drink funny—*Work Hard Not Smart* is an amazingly alive craft book that redefines what a craft book can be. If you read one book on writing this year, make it this one. You'll emerge a better writer—and an even better human."

TIMOTHY J. HILLEGONDS, AUTHOR OF *THE DISTANCE BETWEEN*

"Reminds me that just as writers are not singular beings, a writer's life is not singular in any way, either. The multiplicity of perspectives in Alexis's essays, and her deft, wry voice threading them together, bobbing and weaving from lit crit to braided essay to craft exploration, left me feeling like I'd just had one of those four-hour conversations where you talk to someone wonderful until all hours of the night and can't get enough."

RAE PAGLIARULO, ASSOCIATE EDITOR, *HIPPOCAMPUS MAGAZINE*

ABOUT THE AUTHOR

Alexis Paige is the author of the craft memoir, *Work Hard, Not Smart*, and the memoir in vignettes, *Not a Place on Any Map*, both from Vine Leaves Press. Winner of the New Millennium Nonfiction Prize, Paige has also received notable mentions in *Best American Essays* and multiple Pushcart Prize nominations. Assistant professor of English at Vermont Technical College, she holds an MA in poetry from San Francisco State University and an MFA in nonfiction from the Stonecoast Creative Writing Program of the University of Southern Maine. Paige lives in Vermont with her husband and their two unemployed dogs.

alexispaigeauthor.com

WORK HARD, NOT SMART

HOW TO MAKE A MESSY LITERARY LIFE

ALEXIS PAIGE

Work Hard, Not Smart

Print Edition
ISBN: 978-1-925965-76-6
Published by Vine Leaves Press 2022

Cover design by Jessica Bell
Interior design by Amie McCracken

A catalogue record for this book is available from the National Library of Australia

For Keith, who keeps the trains running on time,
and my heart too
&
For Dad, Semper Fidelis

CONTENTS

Preface: Look for the Plot in the Lost & Found 13

Act One: Become a Writer, See the World!

1. A Portrait of the Writer as a Young Obsessive-Compulsive 27
2. Those Who Can, Teach 37
3. Paper Girl 39
4. The Hero Embarks on a Quest: Girl Writer Meets Boy Writer* 45
5. But Then You Read 61
6. Beware the Writer; Writer, Beware 67
7. Ars Poetica 71

Act Two: Fail More, Better

8. Remembering the Cockroaches: On Doubt in Creative Nonfiction 97
9. On Race, Identity, and Narrative Craft: An Interview with David Mura by the Author 101
10. White Writers' Tears: An Open Letter to White Accomplices in the (Specifically American) Literary Community 117
11. New Fish* 125
12. How About This for Meta? An Interview with the Author by Essayist, Editor, and Luminarts Foundation Fellow, Michael Fischer, about Jail, Jail Narratives, Tropes, and Hopes 139

Act Three: Once More unto the Breach—Still Beginning, Ever Becoming

13. Digging For Mud Bugs and Story Bones 149
14. Lilacs in the Door Yard* 155
15. Writing is Hard, and it Takes a Long Time 177

16. Traveling Companions & Flying Pinball Machines: How to Launch and Land Your Flash CNF, by Alexis Paige and Penny Guisinger 183
17. Rejection Sucks and Then You Die 197
18. Back to the Future: Returning Without the Elixir . . . 203
19. Launching Your Balloon: On Publication 211

Appendix A: Prompt-Ditties 213
Shoutouts from the Runway: Resources, References, and Ephemera 219
Acknowledgments 225

PREFACE: LOOK FOR THE PLOT IN THE LOST & FOUND

EVERY SO OFTEN I forget that the life I want is already mine. When I was eight, my younger brother and I left the Sonoran Desert during the winter for mysterious reasons and Eastern climes, wearing only faded tees and worn corduroy, for it was still the '70s somewhere in 1983. Our destination was Ye-Olde New England, which would become the damp, wooly kingdom of my late childhood and adolescence. My parents had just divorced, and Mom had traded Phoenix for a job promotion in Austin, Texas. Meanwhile, Dad, the seventh of twelve children from an Irish-Catholic family in Massachusetts, had moved back East for work and the outsized support that Catholic broods tend to have the numbers for.

Our new school in New Hampshire did not have crispy rattlesnake skins or tumbleweeds on the grounds, nor, would it seem, a surly pony called Chompers, who our Phoenix school had kept around for class pictures. The new school looked like a Soviet bunker, a low-slung slab of concrete burrowed into a looming stand of eastern white pines.

In those early months, I did poorly socially and academically but easily climbed the class ranks in reading. Like most other American primary schools in the 1980s, ours used the Science Research Associates' Reading Laboratory, which IBM had purchased from SRA back in the '60s. Somehow, IBM then conned school districts nationwide into buying these cutting-edge "laboratory kits," which as far as I could tell were just repurposed shoe boxes filled with printed cards that were tabbed and color-coded by reading level. My grandmother had one of these, which she made herself, fashioned from an old Danish butter cookies tin. A "racket" Dad called the scheme, giving me a new vocabulary word for my arsenal. Maxing out in SRA didn't improve my social capital, but it did buy me almost unlimited library privileges, which I often used to get out of class or recess. It also didn't help matters socially that I was small for my age and roughly six months younger than my peers. Nor did it help that my brother and I had the same bowl haircut ["Dorothy Hamill," my ass, Dad.]; that we were the kids of a single father, which was unusual then; or, that the children of this frozen land spoke a strange, sarcastic dialect of American English, characterized by many missing Rs and insults against one's mother.

In the months following the early ones, I came to believe that my third-grade teacher was either an idiot or an arch-nemesis, or both. I began to openly challenge her in class, pass notes with a girl called Melanie who sat opposite my cubby and had loopy handwriting, and talk too much out of turn. Obviously, these choc-a-bloc stratagems didn't win me friends or influence the teacher that I had done my math homework, but I see them now as the rational coping behaviors of a voluble, precocious child with undiagnosed ADHD.

"Vociferous," I remember the teacher saying one day that winter, to my beloved librarian, about me, in front of the whole class.

When I got home later that day I told Dad the story—how I had looked hard, *right at her eyeballs with my eyeballs* when she called me that word. I had no textbook proof of offense, but there was plenty of context in her delivery.

"What is the meaning of 'Zoscissorous'?" I asked.

As if in our own little parody of Abbott and Costello, Dad said, "Sisyphus? Look it up; it's an old myth." I went into the den where Dad kept the nice books and found one of the encyclopedias, marked "S" in gold leaf, which he had bought volume-by-volume at our local grocery. "Z, not, S," Dad said, as I flipped through the pages, their gilded edges whizzing by.

"Sy-phyll-iss," I sounded out proudly, pointing at the entry for "Sisyphus: Greek Myth." I grew quiet then and read on, somberly, to myself:

Sisyphus: Useless man-child, smote by Zeus, forced to perform repetitive tasks in Hades.

Origin: Greek, rhymes with Alexis.

"Oh!" I said, looking up from the page with recognition, "the story of my life."

My students never believe me when I tell such stories, or any stories for that matter, and why should they? Dubious ground, myth. I teach mainly aspiring nurses, dairy farmers, veterinary technicians, pilots, and engineers at a small technical college in Vermont, where the cows in fact do outnumber the people. The college doesn't have a liberal arts division or school, no majors in Literature or Philosophy or History, or any of the stuff the Greeks might have recognized. I've mostly made peace with this and my role in it: my students simply aren't the artsy-intellectual types (or the rich kids) who end up at the ivied institutions my college roommate liked to call collectively, Camp Trust Fund. I don't delude myself that what passes for education in contemporary America isn't some blunt instrument of late-stage Capitalism, nor do I delude myself that things were any better under Socrates. I've simply accepted my role in a system that has bred and fed me, and which permits me to color outside the lines with enough frequency to sate my contrary tendencies. My students leave with a solid grounding in the practical aspects of their vocation, with some theoretical background, with an associate's or a bachelor's degree, and with relatively low student debt. Most of them also leave with starting salaries higher than my own at mid-career. They don't believe this either, but it's true. Most of my stories are true in their own way.

And the pay's okay with me, too, because I don't do any of this (*gestures at books, pantry office, laptop, five tabs stacked with three open Word docs, farmhouse, dogs, and Vermont countryside*) for the money. I have a lot of autonomy as a small-pond professor, I like my colleagues, I'm still having fun and learning myself, and in an academic market glutted with applicants among dwindling opportunities, I am truly fortunate to have made it to the Xanadu of the Tenure Track. I teach a lot of foundational writing classes—composition, technical writing, rhetoric—because they're what our students need most, but the school and my department are small enough that I also get to regularly teach creative writing, some literature and humanities, and my beloved Crime & Punishment course (which is not, alas, about the novel, but about mass incarceration and the rampant injustice of the American penal system). You do the work that's on hand to the best of your ability. This is what I tell myself anyway when overcome by my own frailties, my own futility, or by the vast and unsolvable human condition.

On the first day of class, the stories and drama begin. "Does anyone know what *in media res* means?" I might ask at the cold open of a basic college freshman English class. [Crickets. Dramatic pause.]

"Does no one learn Latin anymore?" I'll cry. If I'm in rare form I might even leave the classroom for a beat in mock exasperation, or else I'll threaten to throw myself out the window (but only on the first floor). The students don't know yet that I'm just riffing, for fun or theater or pedagogy or to feel alive myself. They don't know that I'm trying to hold them in the filmiest, flimsiest bubble of suspense for as long as I can, before it's margins and citing sources and the exact number of words that constitute a paragraph. (The answer: false.)

I usually start with how much I hate writing. "Everything is hard, but writing most of all," I'll say. It's too early for open challenges, but some of the students will begin to stir, to bristle. Sure, they can buy the idea that writing is hard, perhaps hard for them, but not that it is hard for me. After all, I'm the professor. Aren't I supposed to be an expert? At this point I'll raise the stakes, telling them that writing is even harder for me than it is for them—for teaching is nothing if not a preposterous game of one-upmanship where the house always wins, initially. "All you have to write is one measly term paper; meanwhile, I'm writing a book that is *literally* [wink, wink, wink] trying to kill me."

"Writing is a detestable activity," I'll continue. "You'll never make any money at it, for one." [Pause.] "Thirdly, you'll never be published, and with all due respect to Herman Melville, do you wish to toil in futility and obscurity, only to die a pauper? Dorothy Parker was right when she said, 'I hate writing, I love having written.'" [I'll write this on the board.] "And do you see the comma splice here?" I never go in any discernible order on these tears; I always begin *in medias res*. At this point, if my act is going well, the students are wondering one of many things: *What's a comma splice? What the fuck is wrong with my teacher? Who is Dorothy Parker, and can I switch into her class?*

But I have them. For this moment, I have them. They're taking notes (or cell phone pics) from the board, where I have written, <u>WHAT ALL WRITERS NEED:</u>

- Intuition
- Gumption

- A Penchant for Masochism
- Caffeine
- A Flying Pinball Machine
- A Tangent that Will Burn Up in Reentry
- Other Suffering Writers
- A Sense of Humor
- One Good Pen
- One Bad Idea*

* *Take, for example, this very book, which began as one bad idea borne of my own resistance to cliché and a constitutional incapacity to "work smart, not hard." The bad idea began simply, as a book title for a book I had no idea how to write. In this title, WORK HARD, NOT SMART, I had merely inverted the cliché, and was left only with a vague, cheeky rebellion that would not sustain itself, let alone a serious writing project. Additionally, I realized that WORK HARD, NOT SMART, made it sound as if all work (writing) were drudgery and as if every prose hill were one to die on. And that can't be right, quite. But nothing if not committed, I insisted on the bad idea for a while longer until the effort became a parody of itself, and until I became ponderous, and there was a pandemic, and the meta became the metaphysical, and I was cornered, eventually, by my own brash stupidity. So, what did I do? I gnashed my teeth, I despaired, and then I called my friend, Penny, a writer who understands suffering and who reminded me that writing ain't it. Except she didn't use the word 'ain't.'*

"Dragging for scallops; that's hard," Penny said. "Dragging is the job description." So, I kept on, wrote more badly, or wrote badly some more, and then I took a trip. When the

plane did not crash as I had hoped, I wrote a little more. Along the way, I caught multiple consumptive illnesses and many cases of the vapors, but nothing that would kill me, and I wrote some more. I gnawed off my own arm, tried to quit writing, and then I wrote some more. At some point, some of the bad stuff started to become not-so-bad, and I got out of my own way, and then I wrote some more. And then I got back in my own way, and I wrote some more. And on like that.

Back from this tangent, I realize I've held the suspense long enough. The hour is nearly up, and it's time to bring the balloon back down to earth. So, I sigh heavily, wistfully, and say something like this: "Writing is hard, that's true, but it's not all bad. Sometimes, occasionally, once in a blue moon, if you are really and truly lucky and good, it's marvelous. [Pause.] But do you all understand now why you'll need a flying pinball machine?" Smiles crack wide, and if the act has gone truly superbly, one bold hand shoots skyward, and with an earnestness so precious it makes you believe once again in the goodness of humanity, a small voice says,

"What does Masochism mean?"

Or "Do you recommend a particular pen?"

Or "I think I have the wrong room. Is this Freshman English?"

Kurt Vonnegut says, "Someone gets in trouble, then gets out of it again. People love that story. They never get tired of it." By now, dear reader-writer, you know that all

life and all writing are such conflicts. You put your character up a tree, you hang Chekhov's gun over her mantel, you send her on a quest, she barrels into the belly of the whale, a storm marches upon the land, an apotheosis is reached. Along the way, you mix some metaphors, kill some darlings, posit goals and obstacles, and you have your characters talk to each other and not talk to each other. You don't need any car crashes or heists, for these do not capture the quiet, pounding drama of real life. Your hero resists, someone wise gets a soliloquy, and if you're truly fortunate, you're saved from having to resolve the plot with clumsy *deus ex machina*.

I have always hoped for such a creative, unconventional life, for work that fed my literary impulses and provided the autonomy and time required to pursue said impulses, with a sprinkle of drama in the day-to-day and some intrigue over the long haul. In fact, this is the life I have today, one built—doggedly, steadily, slowly—over the past twenty-five years, and with devotion in the last ten. After emerging from the hard scrapes of my twenties (cities, traumas, sex, booze, and one epic car crash), I began a life of teaching and letters in earnest in my early thirties. Sober in 2006 and freed a year later from the Texas criminal justice system after a protracted felony drunk driving case, I left Houston with Keith, my then-boyfriend and now-husband, for a fresh start in Vermont.

Once settled, I finished a master's degree in poetry and creative writing that I had pursued in San Francisco in my twenties but had let languish. The following year, I began teaching English and humanities at a nearby technical college, and a few years after that I started an MFA program in creative writing. Around this time, I also began to attend conferences, to form important relationships with other working writers, and to publish some personal and scholarly nonfiction. I won a few contests and received some recognition that prodded me on as I deepened my writing craft and practice, completing an MFA in Creative Nonfiction from the University of Southern Maine in 2014. My first book, *Not a Place on Any Map,* a memoir in vignettes, was then published by Vine Leaves Press in 2016. And I'm happy to continue this writing life with the musings I offer here, in my second book, my second born, whose birth plan was fucked from jump.

I should be happy with how everything has turned out. After all, I plotted and plodded my way here. I'm not *not* happy, but as I said, I lose my own plot all the time. And then I find it and myself again, in books, art, writing, the classroom. I'm at my best when I consistently do creative work. And when I keep doing it. And when even if I stop doing it for a while, I start up again, for without the work, I am but a feral creature whose gifts have been abandoned to the Fire Swamp. Getting to the page is itself a journey, and writing remains the enduring drama of my life.

A Note from Housekeeping, or How to Read this Book

What follows, more practically speaking, is my own journey to and on the page, from important childhood influences and experiences to a life steeped in reading both at school and at home, to the many and varied opportunities I have been given. The essays here aim to show the messy craft of life, alongside the messy life and development of writing craft, particularly that of Creative Nonfiction, my genre of choice. Creative Nonfiction, or creative nonfiction, includes many more forms than appear here, such as the flash essay (short-form nonfiction); the personal essay (longer than flash, shorter than memoir); memoir (a book-length personal narrative *from* a life, not *of* a life); the lyric essay (whole books have been written about "the lyric," which is what the cool kids call it, but if you ask someone at a literary conference what one is, you may as well take a hit of acid first); the craft essay (writing about writing); and hybrid scholarship (a mashup of book reports, usually, laced with deadly personal narrative, and even deadlier critical theory). There's plenty of genre-bending out there, too, which I support wholeheartedly. You do you.

This book contains essays both on and of craft. Some investigate craft elements or technique, and some reflect on the writing life or my own creative process (such as it is). Others attempt to deepen my aesthetic development as a writer grappling with both personal and cultural issues of race, gender, trauma, or addiction. One of the chapters is not an essay at all, but an interview with David Mura—American author, activist, and artist whose varied, rigorous work on themes of race, identity, and history demonstrate grit, grace, and courage. Mura was my professor and mentor in my MFA studies, and he remains a treasured friend and "fellow traveler." Another is an open letter, which you can consider a "Hermit Crab Essay," if you like. Yet another chapter is a craft essay about flash nonfiction, co-written with Penny Guisinger, my dear friend, literary soul sister, all-around brilliant essayist, and very good egg. Finally, a few more strictly personal essays appear, which can be read for their own sake, or as prompts or jumping-off points for your own work—in whatever genre or form. These essays are indicated with an asterisk in the titles and a corresponding, explicated prompt can be found at the end of the book.

ACT ONE: BECOME A WRITER, SEE THE WORLD!

1. A PORTRAIT OF THE WRITER AS A YOUNG OBSESSIVE-COMPULSIVE

AS A TEENAGER, when I thought "writer," I imagined berets, rooms wispy with smoke, lithe fingers craned over typewriters, and international intrigue. Someone might have told me then that I was mixing up writer with spy. Someone might have told me it would never again be Paris in the 1920s. That it was 1991 in America and women wore absurd shoulder pads (like lipsticked linebackers), Bell Biv Devoe had not one, but two, hit songs on the radio, and every time I flipped on the news a fem-bot was talking about Clarence Thomas and pubic hair. My stand-out success as a writer had been a paper on *Jane Eyre* that my high school AP Women's Studies teacher mimeographed and passed around to the class. A paper which I wrote the night before it was due and, as always, under extreme duress.

Surely, I had an undiagnosed mental disorder, for I could not simply sit down with one clean sheet of paper and write out a tidy, alpha-numeric outline and then follow said outline as I typed merrily for a reasonable window of time and during which I did not chew pens or sit in various weird bird postures in my chair. As I began the paper (if began is the right word for spending an hour choosing which notebook or journal to write it in and another looking up mental disorders in the encyclopedia), I tore out sheet after sheet of the same bumbling introductory paragraph. The discarded sheets littered the floor around my chair, next to an exploded pen, a thesaurus, and class notes that were written in two separate notebooks and in the margins of various vocabulary handouts. Perhaps I kept my feet up in the chair because the mounting paperwork felt like circling sharks, the floor like dangerous waters.

In fact, I did have a mental disorder—ADHD, inattentive type—but I wouldn't learn that until I was forty, an ostensible grown-up by then who was still struggling with the mundane tasks of daily life. Keith teases that I exude the whiff of an aristocrat who has stumbled upon a reversal of fortune or fish-out-of-water circumstance—he's referring to the fact that I literally cannot boil rice properly, which he thinks makes me seem snobby or aloof. Perhaps I became a writer and later an academic for no other reason than it offers cover for such eccentricity, all huddled under the banner of absent-minded professor.

When I finally went to a neuropsychologist for evaluation a few years ago, the doctor confirmed ADHD, Anxiety, and mild OCD diagnoses.

"Your verbal skills are off the charts, but your nonverbal skills are terrible," he said.

"Thank you?"

"No, I mean, something's not adding up because even with a high verbal, your nonverbal is so low that it doesn't square with your IQ score." The doctor explained that the nonverbal was assessed with the various tests involving digital shapes and patterns that I had manipulated, matched, or identified by pushing buttons on a device that resembled an old Speak and Spell. In one "game," I was supposed to fit falling blocks of various shapes and combinations into corresponding slots below before they reached the bottom of the screen. It was like Tetris, except the shapes fell so slowly, and the controls were so cumbersome, that I lost interest about halfway through.

"Oh, that's probably because I was bored, and so I just [sheepish smile] started pressing buttons randomly," I said. "What forty-year-old behaves this way?"

"Well, one with undiagnosed ADHD, for starters," he said. "The goal now," the doctor said—drum roll, please—"is to learn how to work smart, not hard."

As I left his little office in the tangerine winter gloaming, the doctor smiled wanly as he closed the door after me, as if to say what we both knew that I was going to have to do this—ironically, inexplicably, comically—as I did everything else: the hard way.

They didn't diagnose kids with ADD in the late '70s and early '80s the way they do now, much less little bookwormish girls, but I'm not sure it would have mattered because my dad—my primary parent during my formative school years—was, and still is, of the old school. That first year in New Hampshire was difficult: I struggled in math and anything that wasn't reading, writing, or gym. And since I was six months or so younger than my classmates, with a birthday in late fall, my new teacher, Mrs. Lunkhead, suggested I stay back a grade.

"She's reading *The Red Badge of Courage* as we speak," I remember my dad telling her, his face flushed and angry, gesturing for me to produce the evidence of my prowess from my bookbag. Right after the formal diagnosis, I asked Dad if he remembered this encounter. Maybe Lunkhead was right, I said.

"Who? That *dingbat*? She wore suede, for crying out loud, and lacked gravitas," he said. And I wonder why I am the way that I am.

I radiated pride (and fake humbleness) as the teacher handed out my *Jane Eyre* paper, throughout which I had parroted the prior week's vocab words (ignominy, bildungsroman, Byronic hero), but other than this one glittering paper, I had no reason to believe I could be a writer. I resisted writing, for one. I was undisciplined, only got in the chair once the conditions became so dire that I was like a NORAD analyst pulling the overnight shift. Yes, I was a strong student and loved to read, but my research papers were hopelessly disorganized, my arguments muddied, and I had written only a few short stories, bad Mother's Day "poetry," and some clever mixtape titles. The stories all starred "Alex," a bumbling, suburban white girl who often jogged by the house of one "Sean O'Henry," and who spent untold hours listening to

Prince tracks while making prank phone calls from the mission control center of her best friend's bedroom. At the time, I thought fiction meant changing people's names but leaving the soundtrack intact.

My reasons for wanting to be a writer, too, were unformed, adolescent. Recently, I told my friend Penny about the Tom Waits character in my literature class freshman year who caused me to change majors. He was an upperclassman from Tenafly, New Jersey—closer to "the city" than to our campus at Rutgers University, as he liked to point out—who smoked Old Gold cigarettes and wrote in Moleskine notebooks long before they were *de rigueur*. He took me to a bar in the city that autumn when I was still just seventeen, where he ordered whiskey sours and taught me how to tie a cherry stem in a knot with my tongue. I don't remember who we were reading that semester, but I can still sing all the words to "The Heart of Saturday Night." And I can still knot a cherry stem in my mouth in under a minute.

"I think most of us dated that guy," Penny said, laughing.

"Fine," I said, "but did we all become English majors because of him?"

At the Hippocamp Creative Nonfiction Conference a few years ago, Tobias Wolff gave a wonderful keynote address about his own origins as a writer, citing a photo of Hemingway with Ava Garner on his arm, which Wolff had seen in one of his mother's magazines. Tracy Kidder says that in the 1960s, "Hemingway, Fitzgerald, and Faulkner were still somehow like the current rockstars" and that he initially identified as a writer for the same reason I suspect many of us do: "to meet and impress girls." My own reasons for becoming a writer weren't any nobler: I, too, wanted to be a literary rockstar. I, too, wanted to meet and impress girls. And boys.

Further, I was so averse to clutter and paperwork that instead of writing phone messages for the priest at the church where I worked after school (*Our Lady of Teenaged Hormone Repression*, I believe it was called), I just memorized the names and numbers of the callers. Even if I could find the pink tablet on which I was supposed to take the messages beneath the *Hoarders*-esque piles, I wouldn't have written them down and added to the mess. (Almost no one called anyway, except Father Tom from our sister parish across town, *The Virgin Mary's Cherry*, or Sister Deirdre from CCD, the Catholic education program we just called *Central City Dump*.) Father Joe would poke his head into the office, and I would say, "So and so called," and he would nod through the dust motes and slouch away into the caverns of the rectory. And then I would call around to all the girlfriends I had left only hours earlier at the end-of-sixth-period bell to whine about the clutter and speculate on the movements of one "Sean O'Henry." Years later when I worked at a law office (as a FILE CLERK), the records room gave me the vapors, with its groaning cabinets and files like disembowelment wounds. Ghastly.

The point is somewhere in my heady staggering toward becoming a writer, I overlooked a central necessity: paperwork. Literal reams. Triplicate backups of printer cartridges. Piles of papers stacked all over that, despite how artfully arranged, yip and swipe at your attention constantly. Sticky notes written in semi-conscious cursive unintelligible the morning after. Stacks of books: the I-can't-believe-you've-never-read-X-stack; the stack to understand the how-can-you-never-have-read-X stack; the hopeless-bourgeois-climber stack; the stack to escape from the seriously-you've-never-read-X-and-call-yourself-an-intellectual stack; and finally, the books on your bedside table, the your-mother-doesn't-even-love-you-lullabies-for-self-esteem stack.

So, it probably shouldn't have surprised me when the wheels fell off my already tenuous sanity recently, as I found myself searching for notes on a scene that I had written, oh some time in fall? winter? and which suddenly seemed urgent. This was the scene that was going to crack open whatever thing I was writing. It was the Kafka ice axe scene, which had emerged brilliant and fully formed one morning while I inhaled a muffin and prepped for teaching a composition class. Naturally, I marked its arrival on a sticky note and stuffed it in the back of whatever book I happened to be reading in fall? winter? The sticky/scrap note situation in my life is dire, and don't even get me started on the dust motes.

But even worse is the situation on my laptop, with its too-many and probably redundant files of essays, memoir, and what-have-you. (It's an emerging genre, okay?) Dozens of versions of whatever thing I'm writing live on my desktop, on various thumb drives (and old floppies), or in clouds, all with increasingly hysterical names:

- book.doc
- originaldraftbook.doc
- bookdraftwithBRAIDS2017.doc
- CURRENTDRAFT.doc
- SCENESONLYdraft2018.doc
- ISITPOSSIBLEIAMMAKINGITWORSE2019.doc
- HEYASSHOLEAREYOUEVERGOINGTOFIN-ISHTHISBOOK2020.doc
- and, finally, 2021KILLYOURSELF.doc.

So how can a writer manage all the minutiae and paperwork?

The hell if I know.

I wish I had some practical advice that would change your writing life—the twelve habits of highly productive people, the writerly equivalent of the perfect t-shirt fold, some filing system, a clever mnemonic. But I still have my oak tag journals from second grade. I still have every school notebook, every diary, every boozy journal I ever wrote in—all stuffed into one grandmotherly valise, which I only call a valise because everything sounds better in French. My methods, such as they are, are hopeless, messy, not worth describing—for every good writer knows to skip the stuff the reader will. The truth is balancing a life of writing, teaching, reading, and creating has always felt too hard, has always felt just beyond my reach. But I guess you know already what I never seem to—that the reaching is, in fact, the whole point. That it's only in living beyond or above or past or outside ourselves that we'll ever learn anything, that we'll ever be useful, that we'll ever be satisfied.

My best advice?

Accept the hot mess, make tidy stacks once in a while, chew as many pens as you need to, and write anyway.

2. THOSE WHO CAN, TEACH

"Pursue, keep up with, circle round and round your life ... Know your own bone: gnaw at it, bury it, unearth it, and gnaw at it still."

Thoreau, as quoted in Annie Dillard's The Writing Life

As a teenager, when I thought professor, I pictured ivy and tweed, elbow patches, and eyebrows for days. I imagined brooding, brilliant sirens of thought. Once again, someone might have told me I was confusing NYU with the CIA, for while professorial tradecraft has its own intrigue, professors in the real world, ones like me with missing uteruses and lazy eyes, don't get mistaken for Bond villainesses. Anyone who gets into teaching for the opportunity to be a villainess has my admiration, but not my respect.

I was a writer first, but once I became a writing teacher, I started to use the same voodoo that characterizes my so-called "process" on the page, in the classroom. I used my own smoke and mirrors to get my students unstuck, to get them gnawing on their own bones. Break into scene? We do rapid-fire writing drills. I play keen illusionist to their bored bravado, ratcheting the intensity with cliché—

C'mon, guys! Time's a-wasting! There's money on the line! (Who says such things?) In fact, our whole selves are on the line, and we all know this, hence, the magic show. As writers, we must trick ourselves into *going there*: we have to dodge our conscious minds with sporting maneuvers.

I do, anyway. Each time I write (or teach) I stand at this conscious edge, with my mind's cartoonish miasma at my back—all its limitations and lost points and monkeys and awful chatter. Still, going there and beyond is the point, the singular, impossible point, and sometimes it is also the reward. The point is to hold my breath and throw my whole body into the deep so that others may do the same—whether in writing or life. The point is to do it because others have done it before, and their doing it mattered.

So, I find prompts in writing books or online, and I save them in my teacher's Rolodex. My students sniff phony from a mile off; phony doesn't get you *there*, but corny is no good either. The good prompts mimic the jumping-off point, that feeling of running headlong at the abyss until your breath is ragged, your steps loose engines of wholeness, and your rhythm your own little rain dance. *I remember. I don't remember. I think. I don't think. I fear. I don't fear. I love. I don't love. I am. I am not.* Good stuff comes from the litotes; some higher force comes to bear in the negations and tamps the language into shiny coins. My students fear the surprises that emerge here; they don't want to share them. "That's good," I tell them, "Go on ..." And here again, I am convincing myself.

3. PAPER GIRL

"GET THE CASH for the paper girl," Mrs. Sullivan called to her husband from the landing of her tidy beige split-level ranch. It was 1986, and I was ten-going-on-one-hundred-and-ten, and Dad had bought a similar house in the same neighborhood a few years earlier for $38,000, which I knew only because my precocious six-year-old brother had extracted this information from my taciturn father with the skill and tenacity of a prosecutor during a cross-examination. Always careful and circumspect with adult information, everything cost "two dollars," according to Dad. The price of our modest, happy house in Nashua, New Hampshire, became the exception, the first thing in our lives that cost real money.

"C'mon, Dad, how much?" Josh would ask, about the newest used car or eyeglasses or YMCA fees.

"Two dollars," Dad would say, with a slight smirk. The two-buck tradition went on long into my adulthood when Dad would send birthday cards with two crisp singles folded inside. Occasionally, I'd get a two-dollar bill. Mint.

Mr. Sullivan passed a small manila envelope to Mrs. Sullivan, who made a big show of tucking the envelope, along with some still-warm oatmeal cookies steaming up a Ziploc, into the bank pouch Dad had jury-rigged onto the shopping cart I used to deliver the *Nashua Telegraph*, our local newspaper. In those days, they published a morning and an afternoon edition, and for three years, I delivered the paper every day.

Monday through Friday, I, of the mostly-now-forgotten Generation-X, aka the latchkey kid generation, would do my paper route as soon as I got home from school. Saturdays, I did "collections," going house to house, gathering dozens of manilla envelopes. And on luxurious Sundays, Dad would load the papers into the back of our boxy Volvo 240 and drive the route with me. People tipped well, I believe, because I was a novelty—a paper girl. But no one took care of me like Mrs. Sullivan, who paid promptly, tipped extravagantly, and never forgot to leave her storm door unlocked so I could slip the paper between the front and storm doors so they wouldn't get wet and so I didn't have to fold them in thirds into the clear door-knob bags the *Telegraph* provided. I didn't care about the money. On Saturdays, when I was flush, I'd buy a round of Orange Juliuses at the mall for my friends, blowing most of my wad in an afternoon. I cared about the job, the role, strategy, and technique. Most of all, I relished the independence and autonomy having a job gave me. Being a paper girl was a delicious enterprise that was all mine.

Like my other interests, I approached delivering the paper like a craft. I loved my supplies, my methods, the routine, the newsprint that stained my fingers and made me feel like a man who deserved a beer after a tough delivery day or a long day of "collections." I loved my shopping cart, which was the same model I would use in another life for laundry when I lived in Chinatown in San Francisco. I developed better techniques, memorized the nuances of my route, and timed myself with a Casio runner's watch.

My brief, rewarding career as a paper girl turned into more than a flirtation when I got a job as a cub reporter for the *York County Coast Star* right out of college in 1997. The paper was a community weekly published every Wednesday, in Kennebunk, Maine. The newsroom had five or so reporters, including me, a crackerjack managing editor whose name I wish I could remember, and our Editor-in-Chief, Bob Wallack, who was like a claymation editor, or a character editor direct from central casting.

My salary was $17,500, eligible for benefits after one year of employment, and I showed up on my first day with more than a passing resemblance to Monica Lewinsky (no shade! Team Monica then and now!), with my black, chunky haircut, raison-colored lipstick, and clunky separates. Primed by *All the President's Men*, Pete Hamill, Ruth Reichl, and Charles Bowden, and with the vocabulary and sensibility of a literature major, I fancied myself, I suppose, as someone who in short order could become the ardent, poetic muckraker of coastal New England, the voice of the lobster peoples!

But this was the news business in the late '90s on the eve of the internet, not the Golden Age of the Broadsheet. And Bob Wallack was a short, snarky Bostonian who brooked no bullshit. After working as a city reporter and editor for decades in the Boston area, he moved to Maine for a slower, saner work-life balance. But if I ever said something like "work-life" balance to him, Wallack probably would have sworn at me from the side of his mouth not stuffed with a cigar. I loved and feared him.

Once, I stood in the door of his office as he hunched over his computer with his back to me and grumbling like Winston Churchill, and I told him that I was having a panic attack and couldn't finish my one last story by the midnight deadline, and that I might be dying, and should I go to the emergency room?

"What the fuck is a panic attack?" Wallack growled, without swiveling to look at me. So, I went back to my cubicle, lay on the floor in a plum-colored pantsuit, and cried. A few minutes later Wallack poked his head over the partition I was slumped against, and with no mention of my "condition," he said, "If you finish the goddamned story in the next thirty minutes, I'll take you for a real drink, Paige. Deal?"

I did finish the story an hour and a half later, squeaking in right under deadline. When I came into the office the next day, Wallack came shimmying out of his office like a proud coach, half-smiling, half-smirking and shouted across the bullpen: "There's my cubby! See, kiddo? You did it. Maybe next time you'll get the brass ring *and* the scotch."

He was generous, warm, witty, sharp, eagle-eyed, and never satisfied with the "angles" I suggested. I was just twenty-one years old and in love with Didion and Faulkner and Toni Morrison. Still, he worked with me, gave me crappy stories and murders, and after a year, he even gave me my own column, "On the Beach," where I got to write goofy personal narrative. He supported my tackling of a complex, insidious, and provincial discrimination crisis in a town with a visible and politically positioned queer and gay community, back when LGBTQ+ people were much less represented than today. Not that representation is everything. The point is he taught me some of the best tricks of the trade, knowing I would take them to other forms of writing, and he let me do some of the assaying that I see now I was just meant and burning to do.

"There are some nice sentences here, Paige," he would say, "but what the hell is the story?" When I turned in my very first story on a local Mainer who was starting a salsa business out of his weather-beaten barn, Wallack looked at it and before I could make it to his office door, he was waving me back.

"No, no, no," he said, drawing a big, angry slash through the first page, then the second, the third. "This ain't Watergate, Paige; it's a story about a Mainuh making sals-er. What's the angle? Who cares?"

He was usually right, but I fought anyway. Even when I knew it was wrong for the story, I fought to keep the word "verdant" in an article about land trusts. Verdant ran. The presses didn't collapse. No complaints were made. It may not have been Watergate, but my life as a paper girl was more indelible and formative than I appreciated then. My time at the paper was not a mistake, nor a mere sidebar, for the gig provided invaluable training and discipline to write clearer, leaner, and faster; to think more about the audience and less about myself as I wrote; and to write whether I wanted to or not. Even when I was dying.

he even gave me my own column, "On the Beach," where I got to write goofy personal narrative. He supported my tackling of a complex, insidious, and pervasive discrimination crisis in a town with a visible and politically powerful queer and trans community, back when LGBTQ+ people were much less represented than today. Not that representation is everything. The point is he taught me some of the best tricks of the trade, knowing I would take them to other forms of writing, and he let me do some of the learning that I see now I was just [illegible] and [illegible] to do.

"There are some nice sentences here, Paige," he would say, "but what the hell is the story?" When I turned in my very first story on a local Mainer who was starting a salsa business out of his weather-beaten barn, Wallack looked at it and before I could make it to his office door, he was waving me back.

"No, no, no," he said, drawing a big, angry slash through the first page, then the second, the third. "This ain't Watergate, Paige. It's a story about a Mainah making salsa. What's the angle? Who cares?"

He was usually right but I fought anyway. Even when I knew it was wrong for the story, I fought to keep the word "wedlock" in an article about land trusts. Verdant rain. The [illegible] than [illegible]. No complaints were made. It may not have been Watergate, but my life as a paper girl was more unruly and formative than I appreciated then. My time at the paper was not a mistake, nor a mere sidebar. In [illegible] it provided invaluable training and discipline to write cleaner, leaner, and faster; to think more about the audience and less about myself as I wrote; and to write whether I wanted to or not. Even when I was dying.

4. THE HERO EMBARKS ON A QUEST: GIRL WRITER MEETS BOY WRITER*

I HAD BEEN teaching for three years when I decided that I was done "becoming" a writer; it was time to be a writer. Okay, but how to begin? Writers write, I knew this, but I needed some concrete event or an action step to mark my commitment. So, I found a creative nonfiction conference and spent a long weekend in Atlanta hearing about and discussing truth in nonfiction, reading and writing, and agents and websites. On the first morning home after the conference, and not long after Tropical Storm Irene had ravaged Vermont with historic flooding, I sat in the dining room that looked over the river. I reflected on my new-found intention like a beatific yoga bunny and felt that things really were beginning for me because I was saying so. I was still post-flight groggy, but also abuzz in a heady glow of ideas and the convivial warmth of having spent three days, at last, and in a row, with what felt like a mislaid tribe.

Mid-Fall, Central Vermont, 2011

I pour some coffee and sit in the turret room of our ski-lodge apartment, but the dogs press their noses into my legs and dance around me like a maypole. Teeth un-brushed and slimy, no bra, salt crystals in my tear ducts, *ah hell*, and I shoulder into my coat, hook up my babies, and shoo them through the doorway. *I can't live here forever,* I think, rounding the corner and onto the little stone bridge that passes over the Third Branch of the White River. *Too white, too smothering.* A polite way to think I am bigger than this place.

A larger self, like a balloon tethered to and floating above the whiny one, suggests I acknowledge that I am my own problem—restless, unsatisfied, wherever I go there I am. And each time I am forced to learn this—San Francisco, Houston, Asheville, now here—it is like a revelation, so I'm not as smart as I think.

We cross the bridge and the laundromat parking lot, where a woman wearing spandex and fitness bands high on her fat arms hides behind a crossover-SUV with her two blond labs, past the Chandler Cultural Center, the library cast in Greek Revival; my balloon-self bobs along happily, pointing out architectural details and chipmunks.

I cast my writer's line into town and look around for little tugs, nibbles of insight. The multi-congregational red brick church that "saves" town drunks and addicts pulls me first toward the sandwich board propped out front, the board that offends and tantalizes with its Bazooka-Joe brimstone wisdom: today, the sign says, "A Lifeboat Does No Good If the Drowning Man Does Not Climb In."

The crab apples dot the sidewalk with their smashed-wax husks, and among them a dancing chain of dewy paw prints, bigger ones for the Boxer, and smaller ones, like imprints of baby feet, for our pit-bull mutt. Then something that rarely happens—they both arch over their hind legs at the same time, dumping onto the church lawn with lovely symmetry. *Bravo*, I think as I bend down with my grocery bag.

It's not until crossing back over the stone bridge when I notice how far the river has shifted its course; the backhoes flatten a beach that was just a spit a few weeks before Tropical Storm Irene. The riverbed is changed too, streaked with muddy lines like great claw marks, and I remember the force of the water that day, like muscle memory. I remember the force in my body, like standing this close to a roaring train, like being washed away.

Keith and I watched the river together from our turret, as it toppled its banks and swelled over Prince Street and into the fields of Queen Anne's Lace behind the shed, and all the way down Park Street where the ball fields were sponges, and then past the fields into the little trailer park where the whole town gathered to watch the horror of selection—rolled-up carpets, lawnmowers, oil tanks, decks and railings, old card tables, and hanging plants—plucked like fruit into the water, along with some of their houses.

Late Fall, 2011

When I first returned from Atlanta, I was only flirting with trouble, and not even consciously so. I was flirting, too, with the next thing, the new shiny fix. The location of the fix would be found perhaps in another Vermont town, in another city altogether, in a prestigious MFA program, in a new job—one with manageable hours, a real salary, benefits, and frequent and vocal admiration. I was certain of the power of this next fix, and so goes the illusion: I am always just one more bauble or puppy, or itinerary, or ten fewer pounds away from my dream life.

The solution must lie elsewhere and outside of me; this is another fairytale I have occasionally believed in—whether by training or tendency. My ennui, my disease, my wanderlust, in whatever lexicon, is a cumulative condition, for which I would like to thank all three American coasts, plus Chicago where I was born, plus a smattering of hollers, including the one that Keith and I now call home on another branch of the same White River. Every place I've ever collected mail, or even purchased an airport paperback, seems to complicate, rather than to confirm, the fairytales.

I was getting too old for fairytales by then, and anyway there was a simpler explanation. I had had a peripatetic childhood and parents who sought adventure: I had lived in six different cities or states by the time I left Dad's house in New Hampshire for college in New Jersey at seventeen, and I had lived in seven more since. It was all I knew—this bopping around—and I had mastered the routine: make new friends, meet new people, charm them, stay for a few years, and then when the boredom and stillness creep in, move the fuck on. I had learned how to start over, how to start new life after new life, but I had not yet learned how to live the ones I already had.

The therapist I saw initially after the "emotional affair" I had with a writer I met at the conference said that my dysmorphic self-esteem was to blame for my drifting; she said that I needed to build up my adult self-esteem to deal with my childhood pain. I needed to deal with this pain to release it because otherwise I would continue to carry it around with me like a rock in my stomach.

"It's the black box," I told her. "You know, the one they find in the wreckage of plane crashes."

"I've never heard it put that way," she said. I was pleased with my metaphor but felt no clearer about this release process, nor any more esteemed, nor any less crummy, in fact.

And this was a problem I had encountered before; when my rhetorical defenses were up, there was no getting to the messy work that must be done. I am mostly incapable of accessing my feelings during therapy. (What was it that Freud said about the Irish?) It's not that I am stoic, exactly. It's just that crying in public is literally the last thing I ever want to do.

It's also that I am such a stylist, such a quibbler over process and the shaping and naming of things. I couldn't get past the therapist having diagnosed me as a "love addict" within the first twenty minutes of meeting me; I couldn't get past "Bunny," which was the name of the couples' therapist recommended then for my husband and me to work out our baby impasse. Bunny? I don't think so. Her number stayed on our fridge for weeks, and then months. I never called.

"Practically speaking, how does this process work?" I asked the therapist not named Bunny one day, meaning the exorcism of childhood pain. *Do I lie on the floor? Do I close my eyes? Is there a swinging pocket watch?* It seemed so new-aged, so fuzzy and fatuous, and I worried that role play might be involved.

My memories were tangible (if unreliable). I could have told her some. I could have talked about childhood tokens and images. Such items hold the memories for me—my Mickey Mouse ears circa 1981, my navy-blue San Diego Zoo sweatshirt that makes me think of sea and taffy, the lobster my dad brought home from Boston when we were still living in Phoenix and how his plane got in too late to boil it for dinner. How he left the lobster in the fridge, and I got up first the following morning to find this prehistoric red-black wonder shuffling around on the top rack of the refrigerator. It was before my brother was born, so I must have been a little under five years old. Mom says that by the time she woke up that morning the lobster had been named, left with a small bowl of Cheerios, and I was sitting on the kitchen floor talking to the crustacean as it clicked sluggishly across our linoleum.

I could have told the Non-Bunny therapist this and more: could have told her about the TWA pin-on airplane wings given to me in the same era. I was six by then, but these might have been useful artifacts—the lobster, the sweatshirt, the ears, and the airplane wings I wore on my windbreaker the first time I saw snow.

No one had prepared me for the boredom that stretches between these breathless intervals. Sure, I had had more swelling-of-the-chest moments than I probably deserved, more than I ever appreciated, but there were weeks and months in between that seemed a blur of alarm clocks and coffeemakers and haircuts and mail and laundry, no chic sepia, no neon cheer. Full disclosure: Keith has always done the laundry in our house, mainly because he folds every item as if it will be placed neatly into an army footlocker. He often does the dishes, too. See how little I had to complain about? How much I have to be grateful for?

A surprise collision occurred at the conference when I met Boy Writer. I see now what a cliché I was and also how vulnerable I had been, in this interval of reaching for my next branch: from jail to classroom to literary credibility? Was I kidding myself? Would I make it?

I sat in on a writing workshop to which I was not assigned, and the workshop leader, a muscular poet ("beef cake," my husband would call him later in an uncharacteristic dig) began to read from Mark Jarman's poem "Ground Swell." Boy Writer was attractive and alpha with a soft Georgia brogue: he wore a digital watch, running shoes, a white cotton polo and jeans. He was clean-cut and smiley and spoke like an intellectual, but without pretension.

I hadn't heard the poem before, though I quote it often now, but I felt an immediate and inexplicable nostalgia for its drift, and I loved how Boy Writer recited it, as if there were nothing more important in that moment than to be climbing inside the magic summer other-world created by the poem. Toward the last few lines, his voice began to crack; he read Jarman's words haltingly then: "Yes, I can write about a lot of things / Besides the summer that I turned sixteen. / But that's my ground swell. I must start / Where things began to happen and I knew it" (lines 50-53). I raised my head and was alarmed to see Boy Writer welling up—alarmed because weeping in public was not part of my childhood training, but also touched. I was touched at his vulnerability—his ability to go for it so authentically among strangers.

It made all of us open up more, and these are the moments that enliven workshops and classroom discussions, these are the risks that quicken intimacy, and frankly, remind us we are alive. "There isn't time for politeness," Boy Writer said later about giving ourselves and other people "passes" in our writing, and what I think he was talking about was the danger of the writer putting the social contract ahead of truth.

During a break from morning workshop, I went up and sat with him—asked him something about meta-consciousness and the essay—but somehow we started talking about addiction and mother issues. I had barely just met the guy, and here I was confessing alcoholism, naked ambition, and maybe even a beginning crush.

The conversation did not stop all weekend. We sat opposite one another during a group dinner, talking excitedly and heatedly about teaching, politics, and writing. In my nervous excitement, I ate too many chicken wings, and the proof of my sublimated anxiety was captured in a photograph from that night, with me smiling next to a Flintstone's tower of bones that were polished clean and piled up on a paper plate. Later, during cocktail hour, Boy Writer pulled me aside to ask how I managed being around so much drinking, and then we exchanged notes about the various antidepressants we had tried.

Later, the conversation continued over email, first casually and on the pretext of exchanging work, then predictably flirtier—in text messages and on the phone. Our connection seemed electric; it crackled with the intensity set by a thousand sparks of recognition: both romantics, skeptics, baseball fans, and possible cosmic chrononauts. Around this time, in mid-October, I confessed to my husband that I thought I had a "writer crush" on the poet; I suppose I said this to tell on myself, or to convince myself that a writer crush was as far as it went, or to contain the thing. Keith said only, "Don't get too emotionally attached to this guy."

But it was already too late: the emails consumed me, excited me, fed some part of myself that I had perhaps put aside. By Christmas, we had gone too far, and we knew this because we kept trying to cut off contact. Right before my holiday break I got an email from Boy Writer at work. It said: "A friendship is not something I can manage at this point. I'm sorry." I went to the bathroom, sat on the toilet in my pants, and cried.

I had cried at work maybe once before, during my first year of teaching, on a day I lost my cool for the first time (but alas not the last) in front of a class. *I must be having a nervous breakdown,* I thought as I rubbed a coarse paper towel under my eyelids to soak up the streaking mascara. I didn't understand what was happening to me or my marriage, what I had allowed to happen, what I couldn't seem to stop. I loved my husband, he was my best friend, the best kisser I had ever known, and quite simply, he was a solid human being with whom I loved spending time. We like each other's "aroundness," we always say. So, why wasn't my own life enough? Was it my ego that needed this other contact? My writerly ambition? My restlessness? My appetite? No matter, I would have to let it go.

I had felt an itchiness before I met the poet (not, to be clear, in the form of an attraction or relationship with a person other than my now-spouse, but in the form of carnal cravings for booze, drugs, snacks, exercise, trips, adventures, achievements, and "quirky" eating habits), but I didn't want to admit I had felt similarly restless before, for I was different now, wasn't I? I was ostensibly past the cute ingénue stage—a wife, a teacher, a survivor of depression and panic, a survivor of two months in jail, an accountable human being. I had been sober six years by then; shouldn't I have been reformed? Alas, fairytales hold fast.

Still, I wish I knew then in the early aftermath that I would survive this shot across the bow as I had so many others. I wish I knew that hormonal acne was normal in so-called adulthood, that one might continue to feel like a horny teenager through much of one's thirties, but by one's forties, this usually passes. Enter hot flashes. I wish I knew that baby impasses and sluggish salaries and lagging adolescence were also normal. Whatever normal means. I wish I knew that I was not reformed, and maybe never to be redeemed. I was just like anyone else, human to the bone.

I didn't expect in my mid-thirties to be crying in the bathroom at work, to have lingering self-loathing, or challenges balancing my intestinal flora and fauna, or that the biological clock would seem suddenly like a cruel cultural myth, or an unspoken mandate, an impulse to be visited upon well-adjusted others, for whom the desire to make babies was part of the uncomplicated order of things—school, parties, job with health insurance, stable partner, babies.

It seemed I hadn't been prepared for fantasies about other men (or women) and other cities, even as I loved my own. No one told me that the fantasies would feel at once electric and horrifying, that the million little punches would land.

But they did tell me, they did. It's just I hadn't been listening because such talk seemed too cliché to apply, because I thought myself somehow special. As if any of us is above being human.

In class sometime in the early Irene aftermath I broke up the students into discussion groups about Jon Krakauer's *Into the Wild,* but I felt myself distracted, staring off. I might have told them then about this stuff—the stuff I was staring off about—the stuff I'm staring off about now—that you don't stop pining, you don't stop yearning and longing and doubting just because you have direct deposit paychecks.

We talked about themes in literature, and I chose the book because I loved the coming-of-age themes and the portraiture in it. The portrait of Christopher Johnson McCandless is interesting, complex, full, and in rural Vermont, any text that combines Alaskan adventure, hunting, and flouting government regulations is a win. Chris McCandless, the twenty-three-year-old about whom Krakauer wrote about so searingly in 1996, is a timeless figure, a young man driven by his iconoclastic desires, a young man who embodies Joseph Campbell's archetypal hero's journey. Some of the students thought him brave, some thought him stupid, and others got hung up on details:

"I don't understand why he burned his money in the desert," Marc said.

"It was a symbolic gesture," I said. "What do you think it symbolizes?"

"But then he goes to work at McDonald's a little later; he coulda just saved that money, like a hundred and something bucks."

Some of my students seemed to understand the desire and hunger of McCandless, the impulse toward "great adventure," and some of them didn't.

In a chapter epigraph, Krakauer leads with a Thoreau excerpt, from *Walden,* one that McCandless himself had treasured:

> *No man ever followed his genius till it misled him. Though the result were bodily weakness, yet perhaps no one can say that the consequences were to be regretted, for these were a life in conformity to higher principles. If the day and the night are such that you greet them with joy, and life emits a fragrance like flowers and sweet-scented herbs, is more elastic, more starry, more immortal—that is your success. All nature is your congratulation, and you have cause*

> *momentarily to bless yourself. The greatest gains and values are farthest from being appreciated. We easily come to doubt if they exist. We soon forget them. They are the highest reality... The true harvest of my daily life is somewhat as intangible and indescribable as the tints of morning or evening. It is a little star-dust caught, a segment of the rainbow which I have clutched.*

Perhaps you have it or you don't have it—this kind of longing. And maybe some of my students had already been bitten, but it occurred to me then that this was the stuff I really wanted to teach, or write—that life was different than I had expected—harder, better, more.

The crisis continued to sneak up on me in the early months after. I would be sitting on the couch, say, grading papers and feel it, the deep, gnawing boredom, perhaps the restlessness, irritability, and discontent that are the three horsemen of the human condition. I would sigh and change the channel or get up to fix a snack I was not hungry for. It was something else, this hunger. I had been set up with the myth: first came love, then came marriage ... No one talked about what came in the ellipses, how to manage the pings and pangs, how to navigate the cruel geography of one's own desires. But what would they have said? There is no map for steering in deep water.

For some months and years after, I fantasized about babies, the University of Iowa, about typewriters in a Paris flat, about some other life, and about other lovely postponements. As always, the fantasies were fictionalized and factionalized, parts that could exist only in the neat compartments outside of my actual life. They wouldn't play in Nashua, New Hampshire, or in Randolph, Vermont; these places were too real.

But it was real, my own life.

It was a dark season, getting back on course. Later the next spring, the river seemed to remember itself too, when the ice thawed, revealing deep ruts in the riverbed and great boulders lodged for millennia.

Slowly, the roads got better. Old Camp Brook Road, which had been impassable through November, was open, but it had changed: parts of the road were patched with fill, parts of it fell off precariously into what was then more river than brook. There is no spring in Vermont, only mud season, a season I had never known before I lived here, and the road hazards that March were mostly the typical stuff—ruts and great fields of sucking mud.

All was not well after Irene, but over spring break, my college's volunteer club went to help rebuild a town on the Outer Banks of North Carolina, a sign that there was something to give, and Vermonters seemed to be moving along in their own stubborn, dogged way. After all, what other choice is there but to persist? To shut up and get back to work—there is wisdom in that, maybe not style, but wisdom, and something real—like gutting the animal and then putting it on the fire.

I had not been back on the town's recreation path until one afternoon that spring, when I took the dogs through what was a nicely wooded, tidy trail with a Frisbee golf course before Irene. The path ran parallel to, and in some spots, hugged right up against the Third Branch of the White River, the one that ran below our dining room window, the river that had almost swallowed the town.

It had been six months or so since the storm, and I looked around slack-jawed, aghast at the destruction, mystified at my own lack of comprehension. It was as if I had awakened from a coma right there on that path, to find myself surveying a strange land—a sandy, tree-strewn moonscape. The wreckage had been all around me, yet somehow, I had failed to take its full measure. *Where had I been?*

The dogs were frisky, alert, marking like crazy. The marking was both a reconnoitering and claiming of territory—foreign smells, unwelcome invaders, various intrigues. I had heard that the footbridge over the river leading back to our street had been hit by Irene, but when I reached it, I was stunned. I don't know what kind of damage I imagined (the blows seem somehow more tolerable when you are actively giving or taking them), but there now stood a thirty-foot gully in front of the bridge. Like so much of the area, a wash-out had severed another connection from one place to the next.

Early in my addiction recovery, I heard a theory that we're all looking for a sort of geographic cure, that is, for a change in the landscape that might give us a respite from ourselves. But the place doesn't exist. The fix may be a fiction, but the hunger is real. Geography is always changing—inside and out—whether from dramatic events or to a geological beat, and if we are not paying attention, we might miss everything. We might wake up in a strange land, strangers to ourselves, as I did that year, and have done since.

These were the things I didn't tell my students, these were the things I didn't tell my co-workers, my parents, my in-laws, my friends, and yet they were the only real stuff I knew—the truth I groped for in this life.

"We should insist while there is still time," Jack Gilbert says in his poem "Tear It Down." He says of his hometown, "Only Pittsburgh is more than Pittsburgh. / Rome is better than Rome in the same way the sound / of raccoon tongues licking the inside walls / of the garbage tub is more than the stir / of them in the muck of the garbage. Love is not / enough. We die and are put into the earth forever. / We should insist while there is still time."

The mucky bits are the bits we spare others (and ourselves). When people asked, "How are you?" I didn't say, "Why, I am sifting through the devastation brought on by my air quotes affair, thank you for asking." Politeness, discomfort, and the social contract prevented it.

No one told me how rich and complex marriage would be, how unprepared I would be, how utterly rocked-by-life I would be, then or now, and again. "Marriage is a discipline," a friend said later that year. It sounded right to me then as now. Everything worthwhile is a discipline, a craft—life and love most of all.

5. BUT THEN YOU READ

"You think your pain and your heartbreak are unprecedented in the history of the world, but then you read. It was books that taught me that the things that tormented me most were the very things that connected me with all the people who were alive, who had ever been alive."
JAMES BALDWIN

MY GRANDMOTHER was the sort of matriarch who assigned homework during the summers I visited her lake camp in western Massachusetts. Amateur pianist, autodidact, drinker, diva, Irish Catholic, and mother of twelve, Gram handled however many of us happened to be around with the imperiousness of an infantry commander. Everyone received marching orders, each assignment tailored to his or her interests or deficiencies. Some cousins would help my grandfather set up games of badminton or pickle, some would play cocktail server to a heated game of pitch among my too-many-to-name aunts and uncles, and others made sandwiches at little assembly lines of Wonder Bread and bologna, which Gram pronounced like the town in Italy.

During my tenth summer, I would walk to the town library every morning and check out books from a list of titles assigned by Gram. While my cousins slathered zinc oxide on each other and played Marco Polo in the shallows of Wickaboag Lake, I sat in a folding chair at the water's edge and imagined a gimpy Ethan Frome limping through the dreary streets of Starkfield, or wondered what Atticus meant when he said it was "a sin to kill a mockingbird." Like Atticus, Gram loathed blue jays—"bullies," she called them—and then I understood the difference—for at school I had always been more mockingbird than blue jay.

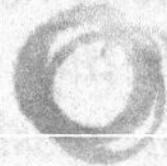

The following winter, my dad, brother, and I moved from an apartment complex that smelled like cigarettes and burnt Spaghetti-Os to a modest split-level ranch about a mile away. Our new house sat on a tiny cul-de-sac in a subdivision grandiosely named Windsor Pond. Upstairs were two small bedrooms, one bathroom, and a kitchen/living room, and downstairs was an unfinished basement, where we roller-skated in tight, dizzying circles.

For the first four or five months while Dad and my uncle refinished the basement, my brother got the front bedroom and I the back, and Dad slept on a secondhand sofa in the living room. At six-foot-three, he dangled off it from all sides, his spidery arms and legs draped over the armrests, his outside arm hanging limp on the floor like a vestigial limb.

He would go to sleep with the television tuned into *M*A*S*H* or *Hill Street Blues*, the foil-muffed antennae crackling into the night. An early insomniac, I would rise in the dark and grab a snack or read and hear his snores rumbling against the hiss of the television. Back then, stations would sign-off around midnight with a long BOOOOOOOOOP, followed by a shower of black and white snow, and not return to life until dawn with an instrumental rendition of "The Star-Spangled Banner."

I had stopped sleeping one night when I caught the beginning of a scary movie about witches; one wore an indelible sneer. For months she terrified me: I would find her under the covers, in my closet, hiding behind my bedroom door. I took up reading during these long stretches of night, with a little flashlight I held under the covers. I read anything I could get my hands on—Judy Blume, the Ramona Quimby books, the *Babysitters' Club* series, an Amelia Earhart biography, *The Red Badge of Courage*, and even Dad's copy of *The Happy Hooker*. I feared something in the maw of nighttime, and the TV-movie witch may well have been the easy symbol I projected to blot out the deep.

Dad found me one night, the flashlight glow seeping through my polyester bedspread, so I found other ruses. I would lie on the bathroom floor with my books; if Dad stirred, I would flush the toilet and go to bed. At one point, I clipped a desk lamp to the rod in my closet and read in there, sitting on an exercise mat with a book propped on my knees.

He eventually caught me on another night, rolling the door open with great fanfare and shouting, "A-HA! Gotcha! What are you doing up kiddo? You've got to sleep!"

"I can't," I said.

"What are you nervous about, Pumpkin?"

"I don't know, the witch, I guess—and everything." He checked under my bed, inspected the attic hatch, and showed me behind the bedroom door.

"See? All clear!" he said. "Now, let's get you back into bed."

"How did you know?" And I wonder now whether I was asking about my reading ruses or something bigger, existential.

"I grew up with eleven brothers and sisters; I know every trick in the book." Once in bed, he sat alongside me and scratched my back until I grew tired.

"Use your nails, like Gram," I said.

"Want me to crack an egg?" he asked, and as I nodded, I began to feel the happy tingle of yolk oozing down my scalp, my head growing heavy under his hand.

Because of my own experiences in the criminal justice system and a penchant for social justice, I try to teach my students at a largely white rural college in Vermont about the issues of race, power, and identity that were seeded by some of this formative reading and ongoing conversations with Dad and Gram. In a humanities course on the criminal justice system, we study wrongful conviction, mass incarceration, police brutality, and how these problems disproportionately impact citizens of color. The white students' responses to the course, set against a changing zeitgeist that includes the Black Lives Matter movement and increased scrutiny of power systems, ranges from shock to disgust to denial. I am most challenged by reaching the students who resist certain oppression narratives, as if stories that counter the post-racial myth are just "liberal" media grandstanding—just television arcs, somehow unreal. For these students and other whites who deny racism, the occlusion is of race itself; Black lives, and BIPOC lives, in fact, don't matter, for they exist in a blind spot, in a place outside of many whites' own description of reality. I am heartened, too, that every year students join the class with more literacy and awareness of justice issues than the last.

I can't remember Gram talking about race explicitly, even as she assigned and we discussed texts that addressed it, such as *Huckleberry Finn* and *To Kill a Mockingbird.* I suspect due to her generation, geography, and personality, she might have thought identity politics crass. Still, possessed by a dogma of fairness, I think recent cultural narratives would move her.

Fortunately, I can talk books and politics with a close proxy, Gram's seventh child, my father. As a Vietnam veteran and retired businessman, my father's interest in race—and appetite for authors like Rankine, Coates, and Morrison—might seem unlikely, but he's a unicorn, my dad. I wish I could talk to Gram about my own marriage of the personal and political, about more books, and contemporary America. I can guess what she'd say about an America of Trumpism, income inequality, climate change, science deniers, racism, and police brutality. But I wonder what she would say about the literary life I have made, and if she would remember her part in making it.

6. BEWARE THE WRITER; WRITER, BEWARE

"My only advantage as a reporter is that I am so physically small, so temperamentally unobtrusive, and so neurotically inarticulate that people tend to forget that my presence runs counter to their best interests. And it always does. That is one last thing to remember: writers are always selling somebody out."

JOAN DIDION IN THE PREFACE TO
SLOUCHING TOWARDS BETHLEHEM

ON THE FIRST day of my first-ever creative writing class as professor rather than student, and not long after I had written and published the essay in chapter four, I asked my students to bring in a writing mantra, like what had been my own, the one above. I like to trot out my shrill inner headmistress early on, mainly because students realize before long that I am soft and they exploit it, so I'd told them they could only become real writers by joining me in a sacred ritual: they were to affix said mantra onto a notebook, "NOT A JOURNAL!" (See Didion's distinction in "On Keeping a Notebook," a classic meta-essay from the *Slouching...* collection.) I read the above quote as students glued, taped, and soldered their mantras to their notebooks, raising my head after with a broad smile, but to my surprise the students looked stricken. I had expected that I would smile upon them with great unspoken heft and they would nod in spiritual communion with the sentences, and we would all just bask. But the spell was broken before it was cast, and I began the peculiar tap dance of a teacher trying, and failing, to connect. On a day when I should have inspired trust, I had done the opposite, even leveled a perceivable threat—I might sell them out one day. No one was safe; everyone was just material.

I argued that Didion's quote didn't give writers carte blanche for revenge or carelessness, yet the students didn't buy it. "Selling somebody out" was something you did if you were a punk. I considered reciting the words of Inigo Montoya to Vizzini in *The Princess Bride*: "I do not think it means what you think it means," but the damage was done, and a dated pop culture reference would not undo it. I doubted my own objectivity then; the words had been with me for so long that I seemed lost in my own translation. I first read *Slouching Towards Bethlehem* sixteen years earlier, while at a campus bus stop in a yellow Paddington Bear hat; I read the book because a classmate gave it to me (in what I misinterpreted as a romantic gesture), and because I was avoiding Dante.

Initially, I invoked the quote as permission to write bad spoken word poetry and pseudo-feminist rants and to jettison the people-pleasing that plagued me. Later, as a reporter myself at a small Maine newspaper, the mantra helped me fake chutzpah to make phone calls and to march up to duffers at selectmen meetings. I covered town meetings mostly, and lobster festivals, but even the small stories required confidence I did not possess.

Later still, the words helped me rationalize writing as astute voyeurism, but since class that fall my mantra seems different to me. Some years ago, I had an occasion to use an insult in a piece, and I did use it—not with particular conviction, or virtue, or even malice. I used it because my husband said it and I could not think of a better word, and as a result I sold someone out. Yes, the choice constituted a kind of loyalty to my husband, but it was loyalty to the story that prevailed. Or was it loyalty to the self, the ego? Perhaps I've always had it backwards: the admonition is not for the reader. It is the writer who must remember to watch out.

7. ARS POETICA

On Deepening Craft: What I Learned in MFA, Confronting Taste and Aesthetics

"I do not mean to be sentimental about suffering—enough is certainly as good as a feast—but people who cannot suffer can never grow up, can never discover who they are."

AS I BEGAN a second graduate program in creative writing (I realize how this sounds, out loud, on this great spinning rock), this line, from James Baldwin's *The Fire Next Time,* hung above my desk —both as an aesthetic principle for my thesis project and a guiding principle for life. A mantra, if you like. My first creative writing degree had been a Master of Arts in Poetry, which sounded much cooler in smokey San Francisco basements than twenty-three-year-old cocktail waitress and semi-retired paper girl. The degree was cheap because I completed most of the coursework in the late '90s and early 2000s when California still had progressively affordable college tuition rates, and it qualified me to teach at "the community college level," which counted when I started teaching at Vermont Tech. This second degree would make me even more competitive in my small, niche corner of the academic market. But more than that I wanted to do a deep dive into creative nonfiction—a genre I felt I had more natural affinity for—I wanted to level up as a writer, and I didn't want to waste any time. Whilemy thesis, a jail memoir, was in part about the "fucked-up life syndrome" (a friend's pithy summary) that accompanies second-to-third stage alcoholism, it was also about the journey of an educated, wobbly-selved white girl from New England who spent sixty days in an improbable place—the Harris County Jail in Houston, Texas. How and why this was an improbable place and how and why that's fucked up is the larger story I hope to tell one day—but early in my MFA, I just wanted to be a better writer, to learn how to tell my stories.

I had a completed, but very rough, draft when I began the Stonecoast Creative Writing program. That version was radically revised with the superb, generous guidance of the program faculty and students, in particular, Barbara Hurd, David Mura, Alexs Pate, Suzanne Strempek-Shea, Debra Marquart, and Penny Guisinger. When I began the Stonecoast program I had many pages of material, and by graduation I had a book-in-progress.

I don't have a strong position on the to-MFA or to-not-MFA debate, which is indeed a THING that you can look up if you don't know what I'm talking about. You could not look it up, too, for if getting an MFA isn't even on your radar, it really doesn't need to be. At one point when the Counting Crows were still popular, an MFA, or a Master of Fine Arts (usually in or of a genre like fiction, poetry, or nonfiction) was considered a "terminal" degree. In that it will kill you, yes. But also in that it was a sort of artsy-fartsy equivalent to a PhD. The idea was that you would study as a practitioner, but still get some academic perks. But now there are PhDs. in Creative Writing and way too many lonely hearts in the job market for teaching jobs. And the good teaching jobs, where you get a two/two schedule and adoring co-eds and unearned prestige, are all gone anyway. What I'm saying is that in 2021, if you can write like Baldwin and you get a PhD. in Creative Writing from Camp Trust Fund, there's a strong chance you will end up teaching a twelve/twelve load of freshman composition classes at Fake News University: Florida Everglades Campus.

In my case, this MFA made sense because when I started it, I had been an adjunct at Vermont Technical College for about five years, and I would have a good shot if a full-time position became available, and a low-residency program made sense, since I was by then in my late thirties and I wanted to maintain my teaching load and spot at VTC. Do I have too much student loan debt? Probably, but I'm just old enough that my first two degrees cost nowhere near what they would today, so the stretch for a maybe-defunct MFA was one I was willing to make in order to grow as a writer, even if I didn't end up with a decent teaching gig. There was a lot of intangible value for me in this whole experience—community, publishing, craft, the rocky Maine coast—but I don't want to oversell it. I was in a unique, privileged, and lucky position in which the degree helped solidify positions I was already on the verge of.

In those two years of study, my technical skill and craft evolved, my sense of narrative structure developed, and important emotional/psychological breakthroughs were made relative to the work. Finally, my growing consciousness around issues of race and how to write about it, especially my own racial privilege, altered both the trajectory of this memoir project and my career as a writer.

The first craft problems I faced in my early MFA studies involved my chronology management, or I should say my seeming allergy to temporal arrangement. "Time management"? I think I know this tune! My writing and scenes, though few, hopped around in space and time with no design, save for a loose associative schema that made sense only to me. I had difficulty narrating in real time (which was connected to scene-making, which I will discuss later), an aversion which revealed even more fundamental problems: I knew the *situation* of the memoir—two years from arrest to freedom—but I remained fuzzy on the *story*. And because I was fuzzy on the story, my narrator was fuzzy too. Which self or persona was telling this story—my self from 2005-2007, with some present-self reflection mixed in? I wasn't sure.

In her seminal nonfiction craft book, Vivian Gornick writes, "The memoirist, like the poet and the novelist, must engage with the world, because engagement makes experience, and experience makes wisdom, and finally it's the wisdom—or rather the movement toward it—that counts." To "remember what it was to be me," Didion says, is the point of keeping a notebook.

What we remember has intrinsic force and value to us, but if I dredge too hard, I can kill the story. Engagement might come in the form of a self in conflict or a time of conflict, but story can't emerge from static experience or a static self. The static self puts me in mind of the Beatles' "Nowhere Man." Who wants to read a memoir about this guy? So how does a writer avoid mere accounting of event? Mere therapy or expression? How does she make art? The narrative forces of time and persona, it seems, make an enormous difference. In my wobbly approaches to time and difficulty isolating the narrative self that would be rooted to the situation and driving the story, I hadn't made any preparations or done any of the hard calculations. Of course, this is what studying and revising are for. In my early revisions, I began to calibrate a narrative spine and self, with real-time narration of events that occurred in the situation, or what I called the A-line, from my arrest until my release from jail. Further, because the prose grew more rooted in time, I wrote the A-line mainly from the point-of-view of a much clearer narrative self—the young woman experiencing and making meaning of the events as they happened. Making this choice freed me to incorporate other narrative lines and an additional narrative persona, who reflects on the past events of the A-line from the present time.

In the beginning of her book, Gornick takes the reader to a funeral, wherein eulogy after boring eulogy stretch on without texture or meaning—that is, until we come upon a story shared by a woman who spoke of the complexity of her relationship with the deceased. The difference between the stories that didn't work and the one that rose in sharp relief from the others, the story that stayed with Gornick, was that the latter "had been composed." It is not experience, even dramatic experience, that makes a great story, but a writer's shaping that makes a story. "Every work of literature has both a situation and a story," Gornick says. "The situation is the context or circumstance, sometimes the plot; the story is the emotional experience that preoccupies the writer: the insight, the wisdom, the thing one has come to say" (13).

The situation or series of events can be anything, Gornick suggests, so long as it's well made, so long as the situation is drawn through a compelling story. And a compelling story—emotional experience, the apprehension of experience—can be delivered only by a particular narrator, one who knows themself at the time of the writing. First, the narrator must be reliable. Much is made of this reliability in nonfiction circles, but defining reliability is fraught. Do we mean a kind of competence, like a court reporter? Or do we mean something else, something akin to authenticity? By way of an example from Orwell, Gornick suggests that a reliable narrator is one who inspires trust by admitting defect, wrestling with mixed feelings, and rendering inner conflict. I came to believe that this kind of narrator has tolerance for ambiguity and for their own unresolvedness—that trying to make sense of one's mess is what makes the work interesting. And true. Or true enough.

In response to Orwell's reflection on the ugliness of imperialism, Gornick writes, "The man who speaks those sentences is the story being told: a civilized man made murderous by the situation he finds himself in." Gornick argues that the reliable narrator must implicate him or herself; it is by the act of self-implication that we come to know and trust the persona of the story.

Interestingly, she distinguishes the narrator's persona from the writer themselves, much in the way we distinguish the speaker of a poem from the poet, but I find the use of the word persona paradoxical. Persona suggests a construct, something not real. Perhaps this paradox fuels some of the wonderful friction out of which stories are made. Of course, as a practical matter, the writer must construct a narrator, a persona, in order to win over the disinterested reader. The writer can't be all of her selves; Gornick points out that our real selves, all of our selves accumulated, are just boring and whiny. We save these selves—all of them in their accumulated banality—for our dear, patient friends and family.

Gornick draws some other important connections between writerly concerns and personae. She writes about style and persona, about persona rising from a kind of stylized, yet authentic, self. As in the case of Orwell, she writes, "the persona he created in his nonfiction—an essence of democratic decency—was something genuine that he pulled from himself, and then shaped to his writer's purpose." That this something was genuine seems an important point to make. The other concerns she has us consider in terms of creating a narrator include distance and subject. She suggests that her own lack of narrative distance sank her early drafts of a memoir about Egypt. She was too close; therefore, there was no movement, no arrival at clarity. I wondered if my own process of revision had been largely about letting more time pass, gathering more narrative distance, and clarity, on my subject. I already had an instinct that writers too close to their story also ran the risk of boring their readers—with half-cocked schlock and drama but no insight—the MFA was beginning to clarify and codify these instincts. Good readers make good writers, and I felt I was becoming aware of this strong intuitive sense I had of what worked and didn't. I knew good sentences; that was a relief, and meant I could move on to deeper pursuits.

Gornick suggests we keep in mind the "disinterested reader" to avoid the trap of memoir as therapy, testament, or mere transcription. She writes, "the shaped presentation of one's own life is of value to the disinterested reader only if it dramatizes and reflects sufficiently on the experience of 'becoming': undertakes to trace the internal movement away from murk of being told who you are by the accident of circumstance toward the clarity that identifies accurately the impulses of the self that Cather calls inviolable." Understanding the *story* as a kind of movement toward clarity helped me to re-think my own project. I did have a sense of hard-won clarity, but in earlier drafts, I tended to swamp the narrative with present-self reflection, rather than meting out the clarity in real-time in the A-line. The journey to the clarity is as important as the clarity itself. An initial struggle I had was giving away too much too quickly, or as Debra Marquart observed, "taking all of the story out of the story." I realized that I had to move toward clarity so that the reader could experience the "becoming" along with me.

Much of this rendered "becoming" was achieved, in a technical sense, by learning to write and stay in scene. And learning to write in scene helped me to see just how much of my material was written in summary mode, and how the summary mode (or its lack of balance with scene) was smothering the story. I began to see also that my tendency to overuse adjectives and adverbs and to show off with language and cleverness made the writing too precious. I was putting these things ahead of story.

In the parts of my thesis, the jail memoir project, that relied too heavily on summary, exposition, and sweeping through common events, it felt as if I was simply covering material rather than exploring and particularizing material. In her book about memoir, Judith Barrington talks about the principle of balancing scene, summary, and musing, or what some call reflection. I began to spend a lot of time revising with this balance in mind, and in my first two semesters at Stonecoast, I developed scenes for approximately the first fifty pages of the manuscript.

In a time when conversations about creative nonfiction are preoccupied by concerns of truth in memoir, the nature of consciousness, identity, and fragmentation, it can be easy to forget about fundamentals like story and scene. Important in and of themselves, these big conversations signal that a necessary codification of the genre has emerged and continues to grow. But the meta conversations can get tedious, grandiose, even absurd, and sometimes we need to remember that readers come for the story and stay if it's well done. Part of what drew me to creative nonfiction as a young poet was the opportunity for reflection, lyricism, musing, and to render a mind at work and play. However, these complexities shouldn't be explored at the expense of story. Simply basking in story is a fundamental satisfaction that reading and writing provide.

As I began working more in scene, I confronted my next craft challenge: I didn't understand narrative structure, not consciously. I had only a vague intuitive sense of my memoir's larger story arc and its smaller, discrete chapter arcs. Working with David Mura and reading about narrative structure began to help me confront this challenge. I must say I still find story intimidating; narrative structure doesn't come to me as naturally as other aspects of writing, so I'm still working out this other sort of *story* (and here I mean more strictly the construction of narrative events). One of Mura's first tasks for me was to read Christopher Vogler's book, *The Writer's Journey*. This book and others on storytelling gave me a fundamental understanding of narrative structure, including understanding Joseph Campbell's mythic Hero's Journey, understanding narrative arc, three-act structures, and the role of conflict and characters' goals and obstacles in creating narrative drive and tension.

With Mura's help, I began outlining different possible structures for the jail story, including the memoir's three larger acts, as well as three-act structures within smaller sections of the book, and I mapped out my story using the framework of the hero's journey, focusing especially on Vogler's understanding of the principle of catharsis: "Whatever it meant to Aristotle, the word [catharsis] has come to mean something to us: a sudden release of emotions that can be brought about by good entertainment, great art, or probing for psychological insight ... catharsis has always been a desired effect and in fact is the mainspring of the dramatic experience." Of course, writing with sentimentality and producing a cathartic effect are two different impulses altogether. My reading of Vogler's thesis is that the writer is best able to achieve this effect by following the body carefully through "the experience of the inmost cave." I would have to carefully render the experience of my past self's body in her approach to trial and jail, and through the experience of the trial. If I could manage this, the reader might experience a catharsis similar to the one I experienced upon learning that I wouldn't be convicted of a felony and that I would only be serving a few months in jail. This release signaled the end of the worst of the ordeal and sustained me through the jail experience, the final battle, Act Three.

I also began to work more consciously on positing narrator and character goals as a means of creating narrative drive. As Vogler maps out the hero's journey, he talks about plotting such goals in a straight line story schematic and in a circle schematic, which illustrate simultaneous principles—namely, that the trajectory of the hero's immediate goals would shift significantly and dramatically from section to section; meanwhile, the direction of the goals more generally would be consistent and ultimately circle back to close the loop. The original goal and the ultimate goal would or could merge. In my case, the goal to "get a life" could morph into accepting the one I already had and ultimately into recognizing that my own life was enough, I was enough. With this work on story, I was able to better understand and more fully realize my narrator's journey from unwilling to willing hero to being the hero of her own life. The circular momentum of the narrative goals could also be described using Alexs Pate's idea (which he shared in workshop) that all writing is about going home; I believe and agree with that. My thesis story was about my homecoming; in a strict geographical sense back to New England, but it also charted the journey of coming home to self-acceptance.

Part of this work on narrative structure assimilated Syd Field's screenwriting principles of resolution/solution: "Does your main character live or die? Succeed or fail? Get married or not? Win the race or not? ... Escape safely or not? ... Return home safely or not?" In one revision, my resolution was two-fold: she prevails, and she returns home safely. On page 126, Field admonishes the writer to "know your ending," which I took as a literal challenge and wrote what I thought might be the last scene in the memoir, which begins as the narrator and her fiancé leave Houston for good.

As I gained a better handle on story, on the thing I had come to say in my book, I began to realize that I would need certain tools beyond craft techniques in order to write the book I now wanted to write. As I read other jailhouse memoirs and more about race, I discovered that I didn't want to write a recovery memoir, as much as I wanted to write about how the criminal justice system gave me a profound education about how society works and about my own relative racial and economic privilege. This desire presented certain challenges in terms of developing a racial and critical consciousness equal to the task, and it also presented certain aesthetic challenges. If I was to write this bigger story, would I be pushing the boundaries of a traditional memoir?

During my studies, as I tried to write this larger story, I, quite naturally, looked for models in literature and pop culture. I became increasingly troubled by many aspects of the criminal justice system as rendered in the American imagination—about pop culture representations of so-called criminals, the mentally ill, the poor, drug addicts and petty dealers, and of course people of color, who make up around thirty percent of the population, yet make up more than sixty percent of the incarceration rates. As Angela Davis shows in her book *Are Prisons Obsolete?*, Americans tend to view the penal system as natural, inevitable, and intractable: "At bottom, there is one fundamental question: Why do we take prison for granted?" This idea that we take prison for granted began to dominate my own writing. And we take it for granted in many ways: we take the prison's physical presence for granted, via constant images, the ubiquity and inaccuracy of which serve to dilute those images' power or to delude us about their import. We take its purpose for granted, purported vs. actual. And finally, we take for granted the prison's effectiveness and absolute necessity in modern life.

Certainly, examples exist in literature and pop culture that challenge these assumptions, examples in which master storytellers have also exposed the reality of prison life: Ted Conover's immersion journalism *New Jack: Guarding Sing Sing*; Jimmy Santiago Baca's memoir *A Place to Stand*; and *The Wire* and *The Corner*, two television series written by David Simon. In these examples, the stories are gripping and the analysis of poverty, political corruption, our skewed and futile war on drugs, and the racism that drives our criminal system is unsparing. Since finishing my MFA in 2014, these examples have only multiplied and humbled me.

I had been growing troubled, too, by the ubiquity of certain media that serve to make people believe they understand the system and the prison, when in fact the real thing, in a telling paradox, remains hidden away from American society. Examples include crime procedurals like my once-beloved *Law & Order*, reality shows like *The First 48, Scared Straight, The Big House,* or *Lockup*, not to mention more sophisticated shows like *Oz*. I worry about them because like anything else that hangs around the living room for too long—old catalogs, dog hair, and coffee cups—we become inured to them, anesthetized, and falsely empowered by their ever-presence. You don't need to tell me about prison or the system, people think, we know about all that. But do we?

I, like most Americans, actually knew very little about the criminal justice system until I was thrust into it. While digesting that experience, and after further research of the system, I began to see how much I didn't know about its vast and complex machinery. I didn't know, for example, until reading Michelle Alexander's *The New Jim Crow*, that our prison population had quintupled in the last thirty or so years. I didn't know that our incarceration statistics bear little-to-no causal relationship with crime stats or population growth. "It may be surprising to some that drug crime was declining, not rising, when a drug war was declared," Alexander writes. "From a historical perspective, however, the lack of correlation between crime and punishment is nothing new. Sociologists have frequently observed that governments use punishment primarily as a tool of social control, and thus the extent or severity of punishment is often unrelated to actual crime patterns." And while I understood that there was a racial dimension to my own jail experience—namely that most of my fellow defendants and inmates were women of color—I didn't understand how race might fit into this larger system of social control. Obviously, I was going to have to do more research to understand these larger issues, and then I was going to have to figure out to what extent I would incorporate such issues into my own work while still making it engaging. For example, once I did understand better the functions of race in the system, where was I supposed to put that material? I was writing a memoir, after all, not a sociology text. Yet, I began to feel called to write a personal narrative that incorporated at least some of this material, especially that which addresses the larger role of prisons in society and how this larger role is hidden away from most Americans, as it was from me.

Without being conscious of it at first, I set out to portray the utter strangeness of jail, to get behind that veil of clichés that stands in for the system, but what about my own clichés and veils? It was ambitious to set out on such revisions of my own imagination, let alone revisions of some [DANGER WORD AHEAD] collective imagination—even of whiteness which would be my ostensible wheelhouse—maybe even glib to announce it, but if my goal was in part to get readers to revise their assumptions, to not take prison for granted, then I needed to emphasize its strangeness and make it somehow not "the most obvious thing in the world," to borrow a phrase from Bertolt Brecht.

Still, I worried about whether pushing further would move the thesis manuscript beyond the expectations for a commercial memoir and perhaps beyond the limits of personal narrative as well. And I worried about whether I could go there: push beyond the traditional form and write a different kind of memoir, one that could hold the difficulty and complexity of prisons in America. I imagined an editor discouraging further development of these sections.

On its face, writing about the racial aspects of my experiences might seem straightforward, unproblematic; I should be able to simply render what I saw and experienced; this is after all the work of personal narrative. The problem in this thinking then becomes the assumption that this rendering, beyond whatever its technical requirements, is as unproblematic as writing about anything else, that writing about race is just the same as, say, writing about writing about events where race is not an explicit component, or not necessary to the writing in question. The assumption of ease adopted in this view contributes to the problem that many white writers face; to simplify the task of writing about race is to simplify race itself—along with a whole range of cultural, critical, historical, sociological, and political implications.

This assumption that race is simple is, foremost, that of the dominant culture's, but the writer inherits it whether she knows it or not. Writers of color know this: their strictly personal events and narratives are racialized from jump whether race is an explicit subject of the work or not. But the white writer may not even be aware that this assumption exists. The assumption itself is hidden, as most dominant or default ideologies are. For example, I wondered at certain points why I couldn't simply write about my experiences in jail the same way I would write about any other experience, that is to say, by bringing technical skills to bear on the task. For instance, I could sharpen my narrative tools and employ good dialogue, scene-making, description, conflict-resolution story arcs, poetic language, and other rhetorical and literary techniques. With flawless craft, I would be able to render the totality of my experience—including my awakening about racial injustice in the system, including my growing disease with a system that pathologizes humanity itself—especially poor and Black and Brown humanity, and including the many-layered and nuanced day-to-day experiences I had while living with women of color, and sharing a kind of cultural, filial, spiritual, and emotional intimacy I had never shared with women of color. A part of me believed, I suppose, that since the experience was personal, even mine (a sort of possession), I should very well be able to translate it, but this belief belies the complexity of the experience. Going to jail changed everything; it re-ordered me intellectually, emotionally, even cellularly.

Part of what the white writer invariably stumbles upon is the fact that writing about race doesn't mean writing about others as much as writing about the self and her own racial identity in the larger world. This complicates things, as the white writer must then begin to confront her own whiteness. Whiteness is, after all, the great hidden racial identity, one hidden by virtue of white supremacy, by a larger, dominant culture which views whiteness as the default identity.

Therefore, and by extension, the white writer's limitations around race are trenchant, hidden, and difficult to apprehend, let alone to examine. In one example from my own jail experience, my bunkie Yolanda, a young Black woman from Southeast Houston, caused a stir when she refused to make her bed in time for head-count one morning. She was tired, grumpy, and slow-moving on that particular day, but the refrain that ran through my head as she got hauled out of the pod in handcuffs was that she brought it on herself. She couldn't play by the rules. She wouldn't *behave*. But according to whom? Couldn't play by whose rules and norms? Mine? Society's? Who was society, anyway? Whoever it was, I knew it wasn't Yolanda. What I couldn't see was that she had her own reasons for acting the way she did, and the consequences for it were a fair trade-off for a small break from the self-immolation and soul-crushing despair that came from constant capitulation to the hierarchy. That someone else's goal, or their very rationality, might be different from mine simply did not occur to me. This blindness was my own whiteness at work, the belief that what worked for me must work for all others, and the failure to see it had implications for the writing. Because of this complexity, I still have not written this scene in the book, though my intuition tells me it will be critical to the jail section and to illustrating what I refer to in the memoir as my "other education."

Practically speaking, to write about race, one must cross racial lines into the territory of the so-called other. The solution on the one hand is to try to know and see more, to read more writers of color and read them widely—from literature to pop culture to criticism. But this is perhaps a superficial solution. Representation goes beyond being able to attempt to inhabit spaces and psychology and language of the so-called other, goes beyond representing with convincing verisimilitude, goes beyond being able to invoke from a catalog of non-white short-hand. Representation goes beyond, too, what are some important, but often surface technical writing choices every writer must make: to tag or not to tag characters according to race, to write or not to write in vernacular, slang, or speech outside of one's racial identity or ethnic origin, to invoke or not invoke racialized others as stock characters or stereotypes. The misleading view is that there is a right or wrong answer to any of these questions; the better view considers a writer's intent, purpose, depth, and care in navigating these questions. The solution, on the other hand, is to stop viewing these questions—and by extension the "objects" of these questions—as problems and minefields and to start viewing the questions as opportunities to explore, particularly to explore within, to explore the self in response to the other.

The white writer, then, should take DuBois's question for her own: "How does it feel to be a problem?" By which I mean that the racial focus of the white writer must be recalibrated from other to self, from observing/analyzing/gazing/fetishizing otherness to examining whiteness. The white writer should find a way to see herself and the paradigm of white supremacy as the problem. The white writer should be aware, for example, that there is a whole catalog of literature by white writers that came before her and navigated these waters unconsciously, who used racial shorthand for a whole range of their own emotional responses.

I am saying that her ignorance of this common literary misstep reveals how little is required of her in terms of understanding whiteness and the complexities of her own racial identity. Little is required of her, of course, precisely because she is white. The dominant culture dictates the rules, and she is allowed such blindness because the larger culture itself is unaware of its own blindness. They don't know what they don't know.

As Toni Morrison explains in the preface to her book, *Playing in the Dark: Whiteness and the Literary Imagination*, this use of Black figures as emotional surrogate is so common among white writers that it has become cliché. When I read this, I realized that avoiding doing this to my own characters of color would be a challenge. Morrison describes an example in an important scene in Marie Cardinal's *The Words to Say It*, in which the protagonist is catalyzed to madness, and ultimately awakening, by her experience at a Louis Armstrong concert, and more particularly by "one precise, *unique* note, tracing a sound whose path was almost *painful*, so absolutely necessary had its *equilibrium* and *duration* become it *tore at the nerves* of those who followed it." The italics here are Morrison's and they serve to emphasize the perhaps unconscious emphasis of strangeness made in Cardinal's description, emphasis that serves to otherize, abnormalize, and make alien an experience that exists ostensibly outside of her. That is until she internalizes at least her understanding of the experience, an experience that seemingly drives her to illness. In this way, in a trope we see time and again, with white representations of Blackness and others in literature, the experience of perceived Blackness becomes a way into a deeper, and perhaps troubled self, and a way of discovery. Thus, the Black figure or the representation of Blackness, is employed as an emotional surrogate, a means by which the white figure might attain heightened emotional experience—be it madness, violence, or even clarity.

Morrison writes, "I was interested, as I had been for a long time, in the way Black people ignite critical moments of discovery or change or emphasis in literature not written by them." Morrison goes on to write about the way that "Black or colored people and symbolic figurations of Blackness are markers for the benevolent and the wicked; the spiritual...and the voluptuous; of 'sinful' but delicious sensuality coupled with demands for purity and restraint." Morrison points out that Cardinal, like so many others, uses pervasive Black imagery as a kind of shorthand, and that this usage carries with it unquestioned assumptions of whiteness in the literary imagination. "I do not have quite the same access to those traditionally useful constructs of Blackness," Morrison writes. "Neither Blackness nor 'people of color' stimulates in me notions of excessive, limitless love, anarchy, or routine dread. I cannot rely on these metaphorical shortcuts because I am a Black writer struggling with and through a language that can powerfully evoke and enforce hidden signs of racial superiority, cultural hegemony, and dismissive 'othering' of people and language which are by no means marginal or already and completely known and knowable in my work." Not wanting to use Blackness as symbol or shorthand, I knew that I would have to write about race and what my whiteness meant in jail. Focusing on these topics for my third-semester paper did not make me an expert, but it did give me confidence that I did have a voice where race was concerned, that I could contribute something credible, if small, to this important field.

In addition to increased confidence, I became more aware and sensitive to writing with a sort of white blindness. I felt I owed a debt to the women of color with whom I was incarcerated to do better. As a middle-class white woman, I had always been rewarded by the world—by my parents, teachers, and even by the system itself—for maintaining a certain attitude. If I worked hard, smiled, and played by the rules, I could get along pretty well, but the rules are made for people like me. Even in my ability to write about these issues, I have been privileged in a way that most of my fellow inmates have not. I've been able to go on for further schooling since my release, to become a professor even, while I'd speculate that many of the women with whom I was locked up might count themselves lucky if they happen to be free at the time of this writing. I might even get a book deal, launch a writing career, and be rewarded for the fact that my story—white woman in prison or fish-out-of-water—sells, while others' stories remain just unfortunate facts, just words on a rap sheet.

These questions related to my own race consciousness then raised certain questions about how a white writer working to emphasize these larger patterns—what James Baldwin referred to as the commonplace of injustice—might accomplish this without breaking form, without perhaps becoming strident, or losing the reader. There exist forbidding barriers against such larger truths.

These barriers exist as a veritable mountain of myth, distortions, stereotypes, propaganda, misinformation, and deeply entrenched rules. In light of these constraints, there is a lot for the writer to take on regarding representation and the criminal justice system, perhaps too much for the scope of one individual memoir, which points again to limits of form and aesthetics, both of which serve to emphasize individual, felt experience.

About my own experiences in the racially disparate and unequal criminal justice system, about the chattel exchange of Black and Brown bodies in subterranean cells that remain hidden away from most of white America, I have felt that the subject requires more of me than a simple personal narrative. Even as the work is impossibly difficult, and I fear it requires more of me than I am capable or willing to give, which is to say, it requires all of me, I must try to do it anyway. I simply must. Prison writers then have an opportunity, or I might argue an obligation, to attempt to get at the real story—to free truth from the stereotypes, misinformation, and problematic representations that serve only to feed a criminal justice system that has gone off the rails.

Fundamentally, I worry that our familiarity and comfort with certain prison images has made us inert in a time when revision of the penal system feels absolutely critical, even possible now. Why was there no great outcry against the failed drug war, mass incarceration, or the hideous racial and class disparities inherent in the system? Part of the reason, Angela Davis argues, "has to do with the way we consume media images of the prison, even as the realities of imprisonment are hidden from almost all who have not had the misfortune of doing time." In this sense, one wonders then whether certain representations of prisons in media and art are partly to blame for our indifference to mass incarceration and to what Michelle Alexander has dubbed "the new Jim Crow." Do images ultimately, whether in television, memoir, or mass media, carry a certain responsibility for our inaction?

Obviously, I have a lot of work left to do if I am to see some of these ambitions through. My treatment of race in the thesis remained uneven, and so in future drafts, I will need to go back and keep developing issues related to race in the narrative. I will also have to make certain difficult decisions about what to leave out. I am no Foucault, no Baldwin, no Morrison; I am not writing the "great American" memoir. This would be just one book, and it's okay if I fall short of revising great societal impulses. I still want to tell an engaging and funny story. Therefore, some of my larger thoughts and questions about race I posit here in the spirit of a larger intention, in my long-term development as a writer.

ACT TWO:
FAIL MORE, BETTER

8. REMEMBERING THE COCKROACHES: ON DOUBT IN CREATIVE NONFICTION

WHEN I TELL people that I write creative nonfiction, I take a deep breath and wait—depending on the company, the response usually ranges somewhere between confusion and derision. Among other writers, real writers like poets and novelists, the thrust might be patronizing. One common point is that Creative nonfiction writers have it easy; after all, we simply have to write what happened—as if the events of our lives come stapled to perfect narrative arcs.

"Lucky!" a fiction writer once said when I told her I was writing a memoir about spending sixty days in a Texas jail. "You'll probably get a six-figure advance and appear on Oprah!" Funny, that's exactly what I was thinking during the grueling months I spent in the third largest jail in America, stockpiling tampons under my bunk and pooping in front of fifty-odd strangers, including male guards. "Wow, I've really hit the jackpot here."

Among non-writers, the conversation might drift toward their great-grandpappy's second cousin's million-dollar story or toward a celebrity's recent "memoirs," plural—the memoirs of Snooki, the Kardashians, or James Freaking Franco.

So, if creative nonfiction writers seem a little prickly, we are. I often feel compelled to offer a mission statement peppered with negations, like the one Lloyd Dobler asserts in *Say Anything*: "I don't want to sell anything, buy anything, or process anything as a career. I don't want to sell anything bought or processed, or buy anything sold or processed, or process anything sold, bought, or processed, or repair anything sold, bought, or processed." Like Dobler, I will list all of the writing I don't want to do: I don't want to write bald confessionalism tantamount to ugly crying in public; I don't want to go "undercover" as a "cougar" and write about the dating scene for forty-something divorcées; I don't want to write a how-to book on pixie haircuts or pap smears. And lastly, no, I don't want to ghostwrite your great-grandpappy's second cousin's story.

The thing is, without the negations, what I do write sounds inadequate. I'm just writing about my life, I might say, and then the stranger will eyeball me for signs of extreme trauma or maiming. I can hear the accusation in their appraisal: what makes you so interesting? Nothing, I will think, and then tell them what they want to hear: "See, I was raised by mole people in New York City, where I ate crack-fried cockroaches, and my best friend was a subway rat called Electra who eventually ate my mother."

"Oh, how interesting," the Stranger might say, then, "Have you read Snooki's new memoir?"

Our genre is shaped by negation. Its very name, "nonfiction," doesn't assert what it is, but rather what it is not. We are not fiction, or as Penny Guisinger has said, what we write is not *not* true. I have lobbied to change our genre name to Nonpoetry, but as you can see, that didn't take. So I say we embrace the negations but call them something else, something like litotes—because practically no one but the odd literature professor knows what that word means.

And there are other reasons to embrace the negations. Regarding truth, I want to make a case not for certainty but doubt. "Authenticity in literature does not come from a writer's personal honesty," John Berger writes. "Authenticity comes from a single faithfulness: that to the ambiguity of experience." That thing we call the truth is, after all, a slippery affair—both emotionally and cognitively—and writers would do well to heed the humilities that doubt can offer up.

Take, for example, Dr. Elizabeth Loftus's work in cognitive psychology, which revealed that phenomena such as false memories and eyewitness misidentification are more common than conventional wisdom suggests. In fact, eyewitness misidentification is the single greatest cause of wrongful convictions nationwide and has played a role in seventy-two percent of convictions overturned by DNA evidence. In one example, Charles Chatman, a Black man, was wrongfully convicted of the 1981 rape of a white woman based on her adamant testimony. Chatman spent twenty-seven years in prison before DNA cleared him. "The most horrifying idea," Loftus has said, "is that what we believe with all our hearts is not necessarily the truth." For writers whose stock and trade is our own and others' memories, this is a sobering thought.

Don't get me wrong. I'm not saying facts don't matter or that the truth is too abstract a thing to reach for. We should reach for it. But we might also regard capital-T truth as a kind of chimera of memory, sensorial detritus, and intention. If we are honest about our lives, we and they are full of uncertainty. Often, memory is not what actually or empirically happened, but the story we tell ourselves of what happened. Or what could have happened. (Or perhaps, if we have revisionist impulses, what should have happened.) So doubt is good—it keeps us on the edge, it keeps us accountable.

Ultimately, I also make the case for doubt as an in-road to empathy. While mentoring young actors, playwright, performer, and professor Anna Deveare Smith talks about how the most important work of the actor is to become vulnerable enough to make what she calls "the broad jump to the other."

"Confidence is overrated," she admonishes her students. "Give doubt a try."

As I think about it now, I am beginning to doubt my own narrative. Maybe I was lucky to spend time in jail. Maybe I was raised by mole people, and it's the cockroaches I've misremembered.

Maybe none of it matters.

Maybe all of it does.

9. ON RACE, IDENTITY, AND NARRATIVE CRAFT: AN INTERVIEW WITH DAVID MURA BY THE AUTHOR

Alexis Paige talks with her mentor-turned-friend, David Mura, author and VONA faculty and board member, about his book, A Stranger's Journey: Race, Identity, and Narrative Craft in Writing. *Mura and Paige first met in 2012 while faculty and student, respectively, at the low-residency Stonecoast MFA in Creative Writing program. After taking the workshop, "Writing on Race," co-taught by Mura and author Alexs Pate, David and Alexis worked together for two semesters, including one in which Mura served as Paige's final thesis advisor. They remain in touch on many of these issues and others. Now, as colleagues and friends.*

AP: Your latest book is called *A Stranger's Journey: Race, Identity, and Narrative Craft in Writing*; immediately striking is the complex synthesis you undertake, even in the title, of issues and subjects so often compartmentalized or marginalized in American letters. The book engages so many issues and with such depth and complexity that I do think varied readers would benefit from it, and I could see it being used in varied contexts, both including and beyond the creative writing classroom. Who did you write this book for, and why?

DM: As I state in the introduction, the book is for both writers of color and for white writers. I want it to provoke discussions in creative writing classrooms, and ultimately, I want the issues of race and identity to be considered essential to the writer's craft. Too often when students of color bring up racial issues in class, they are summarily dismissed as being political or outside any question of aesthetics. Through close readings and through discussions of aesthetic and pedagogical principles, I demonstrate the speciousness and narrow-mindedness of such dismissals and how a disregard or ignorance of the aesthetics and traditions of writers of color runs contrary to any principles of creativity.

To start with, any arguments concerning race in literature are both aesthetic *and* political. As Richard Wright observed, Black and white Americans are engaged in a conflict over the description of reality. Why wouldn't that struggle also be taking place within literature, which is obviously one way of describing our social reality? Moreover, as T.S. Eliot observed, the canon is constantly changing when new works are added that alter our understanding and evaluation of past literature. Add James Baldwin, Toni Morrison, Maxine Hong Kingston, add post-colonial writers like Achebe, Jamaica Kincaid, or Rushdie, and we look at past works slightly differently. For instance, you discover, as Morrison does in *Playing in the Dark,* limitations and blind spots in canonical writers like Cather, Hemingway, and Faulkner. (Edward Said makes a similar critique in *Culture & Imperialism.*) We then begin to see how the inability of these white writers to move beyond a white understanding of race led them to failures of craft and aesthetic limitations.

At the same time, I want to emphasize that this is also a book on creative writing in general; the book's focus on narrative structures and techniques is especially geared to fiction writers, memoirists, and to certain types of nonfiction. I've had students from prestigious MFA programs who simply didn't know how to tell a story. Recently, a student at the VONA writers' conference said that discussions concerning narrative structure or technique were shunted aside at her MFA program. To me this is pedagogical malpractice and simply ignorant. Shakespeare, Austen, Melville, Marquez, Flannery O'Connor, and Morrison (yes, in complicated ways) all use these structures and techniques. So did the ancient storytellers.

AP: As you describe above, the book focuses intently on narrative structure and suggests, perhaps, that cultural understanding of basic principles of storytelling is in decline. Why do you think that is? Specifically with regard to the genre of creative nonfiction, do you think fundamental principles of story—such as positing narrator goals and throwing up obstacles—are more especially overlooked by essayists and memoirists, seen more as tools for the fiction writer? Why must creative nonfiction writers master narrative structure too?

DM: There are so many examples of narrative structure in great nonfiction and memoirs, like John Hersey's *Hiroshima* or Tobias Wolff's *This Boy's Life*; even when the work as a whole is not a linear narrative, certain narrative techniques are used to create narrative drive, as I demonstrate in an essay on Mary Karr's *The Liar's Club*. Then too there are novels that read like memoirs and seem to traverse some gray area between fiction and nonfiction, like Duras's *The Lover* or Naipaul's *The Enigma of Arrival*. Narrative structures can be used to create aesthetic pleasure and reader interest, and I think the more overtly novel-like structure of my *Turning Japanese* explains in part why it is my most popular book.

Narrative structure is a way of understanding experience, not just organizing it. As I say to my students, I can tell the story of any failed relationship in three acts—which also follows some of the outlines of the mythic hero's journey. There's the fallow kingdom before anything happens; there's the call or calls to the relationship and perhaps the traditional hero's reluctance to enter the relationship. There's the start of the relationship which begins the second act, which may go smoothly or wonderfully at first, then runs into the crisis of the second act, the period where things begin to break down and arguments start, where irreconcilable conflicts emerge (when my partner is happy he's great vs. when he's depressed he's terrible; I like my job vs. my partner wants to move to another state, etc.). Finally, there's the point where it's clearly the last chance for the relationship. Narrative structure isn't simply one thing happens after the next; it's understanding what are the crucial events, decisions, actions or turning points; homing in on when the protagonist faces irreconcilable conflicts, when the protagonist lies or evades the truth.

In fiction we create story. In nonfiction, we discover story. A documentarian shoots hundreds of hours of film. That is not a story. The footage must be cut and shaped, must be analyzed to highlight points of tension or decision. A good documentarian also knows how to keep the viewer involved in the narrative and wanting to see what happens next and what happens in the end.

Of course, it's not that all nonfiction—or fiction for that matter—must have a narrative structure. But for students learning their craft, it's important to understand how to use the tools of narrative structure and technique and what they can do for you.

AP: In creative writing milieus—whether MFA programs, conferences, or communities—issues of race, power, and identity are too often relegated to "special topics," if they are addressed at all, or else they get framed as content issues, rather than as craft issues. Your book resists this assumption and argues that considering one's position of identity and power is a matter of both content AND craft. When you mentor beginning writers, how do you begin to deconstruct and reframe some of the assumptions that delineate the ways writers see themselves and craft itself?

DM: In the appendix of the book, I have seven assignments I use in my teaching. One of the assignments is to keep a notebook about all the aspects of the writer's identity that they might consider—race, ethnicity, gender, orientation, class, generation, region, etc. The assignment is based on Michelle Cliff's *The Land of Look Behind,* which consists of pieces that contain little fragments—notes, poems, and quotations on her identity—a potpourri. Cliff was a light-skinned Black Jamaican who had been taught by her family to pass as white, and, after leaving Jamaica, she entered an academic career and was working on her dissertation on "game-playing in the Italian Renaissance." When Cliff decided to begin investigating her own identity, she discovered that she wasn't very articulate; she couldn't find or create much flow to her language. Yes, she could easily write intellectual academic prose—she even dreamed in medieval Latin—but writing about herself? That was hard, nearly impossible. Cliff was also working a nine-to-five job. So, because she found it difficult to write on the subject of her identity, she just allowed herself to write fragments, notes. She didn't put pressure on herself to be eloquent or create long coherent essays or narratives.

There's a lesson in what Cliff went through in writing about her identity. When a writer is just beginning to write on a difficult subject such as race or a personal trauma or a difficult relationship, they shouldn't expect instant lucidity or eloquence or even coherence. As I keep telling my students, writing is a process. You don't get ten feet deep all at once. If you're digging into a new area, you've got to start with the first inch and as a result, the writing may be unformed or rather superficial. But if you keep digging, if you keep writing on the subject, this prods the unconscious, and the unconscious begins to work on the subject or issue, especially if you're doing this writing regularly. In this process, new insights and articulations begin to pop up or perhaps buried or hazy memories, more details. In this way, the writer should approach the subject of identity—or any other difficult subject—the way one might in therapy, just saying what first comes to mind and seeing where that leads.

In the penultimate essay of *A Stranger's Journey*, on V.S. Naipaul, I analyze how his autobiographical novel *The Enigma of Arrival* explores Naipaul's fictional doppelganger, who starts out wanting to write like Somerset Maugham and Evelyn Waugh. That a Trinidadian of Indian descent thought his work would center on subjects like English country houses may seem to us absurd now, but it's an example of how Naipaul's British colonial education led him to denigrate his own background and indeed, to flee from it as a young writer. But as Naipaul makes clear, it was only by researching Caribbean history and beginning to write about this history that he discovered a path into his true subject; his great novel, based on his father's life, *A House for Mr. Biwas*, comes out of an embrace of his identity and familial past rather than a rejection of it. But in many writing programs and classes, writers of color and indigenous writers are discouraged from such explorations or made to feel such explorations are minor, secondary, inferior.

In today's America, our increasingly diverse population is obviously causing a white backlash, and the idea that we're post-racial is patently absurd. White writers, like other white people, will increasingly find that their identity too has become a question—e.g., if you don't align your identity with white Trump supporters, how do you articulate and contextualize your racial identity? Certainly, if you're unprepared to investigate the issues of race, ethnicity and identity in regard to your own identity, you're ill-equipped to write about a multi-racial, multi-ethnic America where, sometime after 2040, no race will constitute a majority, and we will all be racial minorities.

In the course that I co-taught at the Stonecoast MFA, "Writing on Race," we used an excerpt from Thandeka's *Learning to be White: Race, Money & God in America* where she talks to white people about the first time they realized their racial identity. We did this as an assignment for the course, and often the white students were surprised by what they discovered when they looked back to an event in their childhood, such as inviting a Black friend over to their house and then being told not to do that anymore by a parent or other adult. Whiteness is based on a set of rules, practices, and beliefs; for many white writers, to examine the origins of how they learned those rules, practices, and beliefs provides them with a new lens to interpret and contextualize not just their own life, but their family and the society around them.

AP: In the chapter, "The Student of Color in the Typical MFA Program," you write, "In American society, the divide between the way whites and people of color see the social reality around them is always present," and then you describe various ways that these issues emerge in the MFA workshop—often unconsciously from white writers who assert a dominant or default sense of taste or subjectivity they aren't even aware of as such. And yet, it happens, and in fact, it happens so predictably that students of color can expect to experience certain classic encounters; this chapter reads, in part, as a survival manual written for these students of color. What do MFA programs need to do or do better to begin to right these imbalances and take responsibility for all students' experiences in the MFA? What do teachers in MFA programs need to do to address these problems so that students of color can enjoy and thrive, rather than survive, their MFA studies?

DM: In another essay in the book, "Writing Teachers—or David Foster Wallace vs. James Baldwin," I argue that MFA programs need to address the willed ignorance of certain white professors—their lack of knowledge of the work and craft of writers of color. Obviously, these professors can't open up their booklists or teach to a wider and more diverse set of works and aesthetic principles if they aren't aware of this diversity. Then too, there's an intellectual tradition and a historical background that's needed to properly interpret and contextualize the works of writers of color—Toni Morrison's *Playing in the Dark*, bell hooks' essays, Edward Said's *Orientalism* and *Culture and Imperialism*, Baldwin's *The Price of the Ticket,* Henry Louis Gates, Jr.'s *The Signifying Monkey*, etc.; Marxist criticism, feminist criticism, GBLT criticism, scholars like Claude Steele on stereotype consciousness and stereotype threat ... this list could go on and on.

This preparation involves simply reading more widely. But the white writer or professor who has not read in these traditions must also ask themselves why; what are the prejudices and white-identified concepts which have led to their ignorance? And beyond that, they must engage in a psychological and spiritual reorientation of their own identity.

For one thing, white ignorance of the works of people of color often inherently assumes—consciously or unconsciously—that these works are inferior. Of course, this assumption is racist, but that is precisely why these tasks are so difficult. White writer professors are liberals; they want to think of themselves as enlightened and innocent. To confront their own prejudices and ignorance, they must abandon and deconstruct that sense of innocence. And this is no simple task.

As Baldwin observed, "The question of identity is a question involving the most profound panic—a terror as primary as the nightmare of the mortal fall." And yet, not to engage such a question, Baldwin argues in "Stranger in the Village," creates its own problems: "People who shut their eyes to reality invite their own destruction, and anyone who insists on remaining in a state of innocence long after that innocence is dead turns himself into a monster." Now let me be clear: I'm not saying that these white writing teachers are monsters; what I am saying is that Baldwin's statement here surely applies to this country and our culture as a whole when it comes to issues of race.

The task of opening up MFA programs and making them more conducive to the work and presence of writers of color is not an easy one. Why would it be? We've been dealing with racism in this country from the time of its inception and we are still a divided people racially. Again, why would we expect the world of letters to be any different?

AP: "The work will teach you how to do the work," you reminded me on the phone recently. "Do whatever it takes to keep the writing going; you'll write your way into the answers that you need." How or when in the process of writing this book did you know that race, identity, and narrative craft were all part of one book? Did you set out to write about them all, or did they come together by way of alchemy in the writing itself?

DM: In much earlier incarnations, the book was rejected by two publishers. At the time, I was of course disappointed and discouraged by this; I experienced that sense of failure and even despair that I describe in the book as part of certain narrative constructions—the crisis of the second act of a three-act play; this is the dark night of the soul that comes in the middle of the mythical hero's journey. Still, I continued working on the book because it came out of questions and problems that I encountered with students in my teaching at the VONA writers' conference and in the Stonecoast MFA program.

At Stonecoast, I was writing long letters to individual students about their work, and I found that, unlike in many workshops, it wasn't enough for me simply to point out the problems or deficiencies in their work. I had to help them come up with possible solutions or new ways of considering and addressing those problems and deficiencies. In this way I never stopped working on the book; I made it part of my job as a teacher.

I also kept in mind a couple bromides about writing. As I've said to you, "You can always revise something; you can't revise nothing." Just write something; it doesn't have to be perfect; writing is a process. I was also fueled by my friend Garrett Hongo's observation after reading through drafts of *Turning Japanese*, my first memoir: "David, you're not a writer, you're a rewriter." To put it more bluntly, he was saying, David, your first drafts are shit, but you just keep working at the writing and revising and eventually you get it.

The connections in the book among race, identity, narrative craft, and the process of becoming a writer stems from both my teaching and my own writing. For instance, in the essay on the four questions regarding the narrator, the opening question is: Who is the narrator? This question applies to memoir in an obvious way, but it applies even to the third-person omniscient narrator in fiction. So the very first question regarding narration involves these issues of identity. And so does the second, whom is the narrator telling the story to?

Let me take just one aspect of this second question. As Toni Morrison has observed, until very recently, white American writers never imagined a Black reader; that is, white writers didn't feel they had to consider how a Black readership might interpret and evaluate their writing. Writers of color know that the literary gatekeepers will often be white. As I say in the book, that doesn't mean a POC writer needs to write for a white audience, but we are certainly aware that our work will be judged by a white audience. Indeed, that actually involves, as DuBois noted, a more complex dual and multiple consciousness. But today, as opposed to the past, white writers must understand that those who read and judge their work will increasingly not be white; often, those readers and writers of color and indigenous writers may look at your writing differently than you do—so why would you want to remain ignorant of different aesthetics and ways of approaching writing? In her introduction to *The Best American Short Stories 2018*, Roxane Gay delineates her aesthetic disagreements with the choices of Richard Russo in an earlier edition.

This is not to say that Gay is right and Russo wrong, but to say that you can't even evaluate their differences if you aren't aware of how Gay is formulating her aesthetic criteria.

Of course, with students of color, it's often obvious to them that their racial and/or ethnic identity is a multi-faceted question, but this is also true for white writers. American culture itself emphasizes the individual over the group, but it's clear that we are simultaneously individuals and members of a group. Moreover, in part because of this cultural tendency—and in part because of the ways race is processed, or rather, denied in this country—my students, but particularly white students, often had a hard time thinking of themselves as a member of a group or how the lens of the group comes in many different contexts—race, ethnicity, class, gender, orientation, generation, region, history, etc.

AP: I remember well my own resistance. Thinking about these issues is work—some of the hardest and best kind—

but still work, and ongoing, endlessly complex. As a white writer, I have more work ahead of me than I can ever fully appreciate, for as you say, we don't know what we don't know. Such realizations can be daunting. In our semesters together, for example, I would often hope that some evolving draft was, if not done, then at least getting close—only to find one of your legendary letters in my inbox about more that needed to be done, or that could be done, or about different frameworks to consider, different ways of thinking that might open up the work, ways to formulate my own aesthetic criteria. With the single-mindedness of all students, I began to worry about ever finishing anything: "What if I can't finish it?" I asked you about my thesis. "The thesis will teach you how to finish it," you said. I loved this idea, still love this idea—that the work is itself instructive—that the work is animate even; it decides, not the writer. What a relief! Now, on my best writing days, I am able to get out of the way and listen to the work. What did this book teach you as you wrote it?

DM: First off, I learned that history and reality can change rapidly and thus, the context around your own work. Here's how the book opens: "The earliest essays in this book were written just before Barack Hussein Obama was elected President, bringing some deluded people to declare a post-racial America. I write this introduction just after the 2016 election, in a nation where Michael Brown and Ferguson, Freddie Gray, Baltimore and Black Lives Matter are now juxtaposed against the rampant racism, xenophobia, religious bigotry, and sexism of Donald Trump's election."

I started the book in a time when many white writers did not want to think about the issues of race or thought them as mainly part of the past. In Trump's America, race—and thus the question of white identity—cannot be avoided. So I started the book in a climate where I felt my project was a steep, uphill climb, and now I feel the book has come out at a time when the issues related to race are more and more considered a necessary part of our literary conversation. In short, I've gone from being ahead of the curve to just keeping up with it. That's why I'm rushing to finish my next book of essays on race.

As I mentioned earlier, the readers for the University of Georgia Press asked for more material about race and identity. I was also spurred on by conversations with students and writers of color about their experiences in creative writing classrooms. In the process, I've had to work towards a deeper understanding of how race structures our perceptions of our social reality, and thus, how literature is created and interpreted. If unconscious or implicit bias is at work in other areas of society, why wouldn't it also infect our considerations of literary craft and excellence?

And what are the sources of that bias? Over the last twenty-five years, the scholarship and theory concerning race has exploded, and I've tried to keep up with that—Frank Wilderson, Saidiya Hartman, Khalil Gibran Mohammad, Michelle Alexander, Critical Race Theory.

I've also had to become less concerned about negative reactions to what I'm saying about race and literature, and this has been bolstered by finding the intellectual and literary arguments to support my views. As I say a couple times in my book, *we start to write a book in order to become the person who finishes the book.* I sometimes tell people, "I'm a Japanese-American kid who grew up white-identified in a Jewish suburb of Chicago." When a white friend would say to me, "David, I think of you as a white person," that was the way I wanted to be regarded.

That kid still resides in me and he's astonished at what I'm now writing, what my life—so much more diverse than when I was growing up—has become.

10. WHITE WRITERS' TEARS: AN OPEN LETTER TO WHITE ACCOMPLICES IN THE (SPECIFICALLY AMERICAN) LITERARY COMMUNITY

Dear Writers of the Caucasian Persuasion,

I have to confess something: I am racist. You probably are too. All white people are, even the "good" ones, for we have all been socialized in an overtly racist system of structures and super structures. This acknowledgment matters, but what matters more is what we do with it. What matters is that we rise and meet the challenges of this and future American moments, and that we see them as opportunities to be better—perhaps even to be great—for despite what the politicians say, America has never been and is not now a "great" place for *everyone*.

I have internalized white supremacist narratives, as we all have—and here I do mean "we" across racial lines. Systems and power structures favor me, whether in housing and employment; whether on the street; in department stores; restaurants; classrooms; hospitals; on airplanes and in taxis; in the criminal justice system; in professional and academic spaces; and *here*, in the literary universe that not everyone can call home with the same certainty and safety. Here, we stand at the precipice of something enormous—that is, our history, and just as malignant, ourselves. Our own performance of white supremacy is an abyss I hope we look hard and long into. I want to suggest that we increase our tolerance for discomfort, that we ditch the phony benevolence that Claudia Rankine described in her AWP 2016 keynote address. (Benevolence was her word, phony mine.) That we get over ourselves and out of the way enough to dig into the work of achieving real racial equity (*equity*, an emphasis I am borrowing from writer Jen Palmares Meadows who posited it as a better alternative to mere *diversity*).

Such work of inclusion might not seem like life and death here in this literary bubble, but out there in the world, people are dying—and the stories we tell in here become the stories that exist in the world. The power systems and structures and hierarchies that exist here in this purportedly inclusive space of mostly good, "benevolent" liberals, conscious folks, and thinkers who know how to use words like "intersectional" are *exactly the same* systems and structures and hierarchies that exist out in the world where:

- Voter disenfranchisement disproportionately impacts men of color;

- Housing and employment discrimination disproportionately impacts people of color, as well as those of other marginalized identities;
- People of color make up about thirty percent of the population, yet sixty percent of those incarcerated;
- Black teens are (according to one report) twenty-one times more likely to be shot dead by police than their white counterparts;
- Renisha McBride knocked on a door for help after a car accident and was promptly shot in the face by a white man who saw her—whether immediately or consciously or unconsciously—as a threat. His intent doesn't matter because his not meaning to, his remorse, and his apology do not make Renisha McBride less dead.
- Someone like me, a good, "benevolent" white middle-class girl with high-class problems, can blunder colossally, yet still have a real second chance after alcoholism/a drunk driving arrest/a felony charge/ and two months in the Harris County Jail—while my bunkie, Yolanda, a Black woman my age from Sunnyside in Houston, barely got a first chance.
- And someone like me had access and the financial wherewithal to hire good legal representation, and therefore, remained free on bond for one year and nine months—while Yolanda languished in the deplorable Harris County jail for eighteen months awaiting trial on a trumped-up drug charge that was ultimately dismissed and on another charge called "criminal mischief," which sounds suspiciously like a made-up term for something/ anything to charge Black people with.

While I was out on bond getting treatment for alcoholism, Yolanda remained in a jail so foul with corruption and violence and sexual assaults and disease and rats and roaches that many of you would *literally* not believe it, a nightmarish, and yet commonplace, place that no one should have to endure and that seasoned inmates there refer to as the "slave ship." You might not be able to hold the truth of this other America in your body, the America that you perhaps don't know, because unlike our Black and Brown sisters, you don't live *in* it and *with* it and *of* it *every fucking day*. And regardless of good intentions, our literary world is fundamentally the same as the space out there, where after a trial and only a misdemeanor conviction, and "no paper" (probation or parole), and the resources to do so, I was able to live my second chance, to leave the state of Texas and to move on to Vermont, where I am now a professor and homeowner. While Yolanda revolves in and out of prison for an originally-nonsense charge because she can't keep up with the onerous court conditions that make parole violations inevitable, I have retained—even expanded—my life of privilege and comfort.

I took the long way around with this object lesson, but I reiterate, the world in here looks and acts just like the one out there. Here, whites are overrepresented on panels and mastheads and in departments and journals and fellowships and prizes, and MFA programs don't teach and reflect the plurality of narratives that actually exist in both the literary world and the actual world. And even though probably no one is going to get shot in broad daylight on the steps of the Acme City Convention Center during this Association of Writers and Writing Program's, let's not kid ourselves that the world of American letters is for everyone a place of safety, justice, and equity. But isn't this what we want—what *we* all want? We want inclusion, right?

We say we do, but as the brilliant and fabulous poet and activist Amanda Johnston posted on social media recently, "PSA: Listen closely to people's actions." So while I have done a lot of homework in changing my framework for thinking about race and my own privilege, and while I write and teach to these principles, I have not always acted upon them perfectly. I want you to listen closely to these actions, my actions:

- I have not always sacrificed my privilege at work, in literary spaces, in my MFA, and in publishing in order to center the wellbeing of writers of color.
- I have centered myself and my white feelings in conversations where people of color had to do both their own and my heavy lifting. I have added to their labor.
- I have not always given up my seat at the table.
- I take breaks—days and weeks off—from engaging race (as if an entity that lives outside of me)—whether on social media, in the classroom, or on the page. And I do this because engaging is hard, but more so because as a white writer/editor/teacher, *I can*. I have the ability and privilege to disengage.
- I have also failed to share or cede both space and power in literary spaces.

Let me give you a concrete example:

Many years ago now, I was involved in a project that ended up being (see, I say "ended up," as if it were passive, as if choices weren't made) a collection of mostly white voices. An implosion among contributors occurred after someone pointed this out, and a somewhat predictable, ugly conversation ensued. Some asked whether it was enough to solicit writers of color and to publish calls in national venues (which was done—and with good intention and sincere effort—by the editor of the project). If such efforts fail, does further editorial responsibility still exist to actively and decisively include non-white writers in meaningful proportions? My answer was and is yes. Part of what made the implosion sticky was that friendships were involved, and feelings were hurt, as I and others tried to engage in an honest discussion of intersectionality and inclusions. (Social-justice-warrior points for me! Where's my cookie?) However, what I did not *do* was withdraw my piece from the collection. After all, it was an excellent project in all other respects, and I wanted to be in it—to stack up my publication credits—I wanted that more than I wanted to insist on the inclusion of non-normative voices. So I vowed to do better ... next time. Next time, I would join only projects and publications that were specifically committed to meaningful inclusion of writers of color no matter what.

But guess what? I did do it again. I joined another project whose racial composition shaped up to be mostly white. Of course, I had good reasons for my involvement in this project, too, but were they the right reasons?

I don't relish being a slow learner on this front, nor that, once again, I was promising to do better next time. Therefore, I want to make my vow public here, and I want to entreat other white writers to do the same. What does doing better look like? What might I do next time? What can we white writers do to sincerely foster inclusion and better support writers of color?

We can:

- Refuse solicitations to projects that lack meaningful inclusions, and we can (and should) tell the editors and publishers why;
- Demand fair and meaningful representation of writers of color as a condition of participation;
- Call out, ask for, and demand accountability of publishing statistics by race (e.g., the VIDA count on gender, which I realize is beginning to include race and other metrics);
- Resist and reject essentialist white narratives in our own writing and in our roles as editors of various publications;
- Give up our seats at certain tables, or create additional seats for BIPOC writers;
- Work to make sure mastheads are not all or mostly white or inclusive merely in a tokenizing way;
- Share and yield opportunities to speak, to publish, to perform, to panel, to get paid, etc., to writers of color;
- As the novelist, poet, memoirist, and activist Alexs Pate has said, cross the street to come to the aid of people of color who are under attack;

- Take on the labor (which people of color now do) of educating other whites to become more conscious, sensitive, and inclusive;
- And finally, help to reframe narratives in our writing, teaching, editing, and publishing, so as to improve the narratives here and in other spaces.

We can do better. We must.

11. NEW FISH*

May 5, 2005, Houston Southeast City Jail

THE BLANKETS are "at laundry," the guards say. Some of the other inmates grouse at the news. "Like we just fuckin' animals," one girl says and then slams the fleshy side of her fist into the Plexiglas opposite the guard picket, leaving a sweaty hologram like one of those baby feet prints Josh and I used to make on the inside of Dad's frosted hatchback. I am tempted to walk over and dot five little toes in an arc over the print before it fades, and the thought forms a sad lozenge in my throat. The guards ignore us, but it's a studied nonchalance, sadistic and mirthful.

"Shhhhhhh!" I scream inside, thinking it can't be good to piss them off, better to be sycophantically polite. I am so white.

We are in a communal holding cell, where about fifty of us sit at a cafeteria table in front of our middle-of-the-night breakfast trays. We are in miniskirts and stretchy knits, in soiled jeans and Goodwill t-shirts: we are bloodied, stricken, wigs akimbo—all of our night-filth naked to fluorescence. The table is god's waiting room:

here we sit together, passing stories and powdered eggs. The meaty part of my upper arm oozes blood from a two-inch gash, what will later be the one physical scar I sustain, and my thighs and knees ache from the crash, the blood now a dark syrup that stiffens my jeans. From my tray, I drink thick fruit punch from a disposable cup with a foiled lid but avoid the pale spitballs of scrambled eggs. A lanky Black girl, who reminds me of Big Bird with her fried-blonde-turned-yellow hair and her huge Muppet hands, asks what happened.

"I dunno," I offer. "Car accident," I say, then tell her I was arrested for drunk driving.

"No shit," she says. "Hope you didn't kill no one."

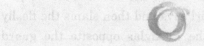

If only I knew. If only I could figure out that central thing that drove me here. These reckonings always squared me against the larger thing, where for a moment I would be alone, repentant, promising to do better, only to squirm away again. If only I could figure out the thing first. Practically speaking, I drove me here. Yes. In a jeep. And then the police drove me here, here, from the crash. But what ugliness or wrongness compelled me to these ever-worse troubles, these ever more dangerous waters? Was I testing, looking for further proof? The dark thing that gnawed me from my marrow: I wanted its name.

I do not remember my first drink: it was either a Fuzzy Navel in my best friend's laundry room, or it was a White

Russian in my parents' kitchen. It doesn't matter, but the accounting is compulsive, a futile effort to control the thing. I can't remember how many I had before the crash. I lost count, but I gave the cop a number. I can't now remember the number. Reasonable might have been two or three, but if two or three was the number I gave, it was a lie. I never have just two or three anymore. I must stop drinking, I know this, but I push the thought away.

I should be transported to County any minute now—where I will stay today, tonight, the next, forever, who-the-fuck-knows-how-long, my future like a horizon that unravels in my body. I sit with my back to the guards and facing my fellow arrestees, across from a chubby blonde who keeps burping up on herself after some fascinating head lolling; the rest of us watch her—partly out of boredom, partly to duck projectiles. I've seen a lot of drunkenness as a bartender, but never someone quite so possessed, never someone quite so committed to being an absolute mess, and yet, I watch her as much with recognition as horror. I know this head-wagging, barfy, lilting nonsense state of oblivion. This is the place I set out to nearly every time I drink in recent memory. Off to oblivion, I imagine myself announcing at some portal of insanity; see you if I get back! It's just cheap comfort, but comfort nonetheless, to laugh as others taunt her, to partake of the schadenfreude that provides false distance from the self. I might be a little bruised and bloodied, but at least I'm not covered in puke.

I am from a quote-unquote good middle-class family, which is to say that I am a white, college-educated woman with access to the privilege of my packaging, including the expectation that I would never see the inside of a jail. On paper, I am a white girl from Chicago and Phoenix and Texas and New Hampshire. I moved to Houston last year, where my younger brother, Josh, goes to college, with a vague idea that together we would beat our mutual malaise. Our rescue plan didn't go very far: we thought we might get an apartment on Richmond Avenue and watch *Beverly Hills Cop* and *Planes, Trains and Automobiles* and recite the words to each other like childhood koans, and everything would get better, as if by sibling-bonded osmosis. But by the time I arrive, I am waist-deep in Champagne and tequila and unable to leave its vapors, and Josh toes around the edges, shiftless and bored. I am still working in the bar biz, as I have done for the last eight years since college, but "At least I'm a manager!" I tell myself. "And I'm writing!" (Never mind that it's just a hucksterish wine marketing newsletter.)

Alcohol encircled me subtly and, at first, slowly. Busy with sports and grades and the college prep rat race, I didn't bother much with drinking in high school, or in college, where I was busy trying to get that one Tom Waits character in my English class (for there was always one) to look my way. I did not have the early, stomach-pumping alcoholic experience that many of my fellows in recovery now point to with hindsight clarity.

I started drinking in earnest when I moved to San Francisco a couple of years after college in 1999. Primed by a strange admixture of Rat Pack movies, pulp fiction and too much Didion and 1980s *Vogue* magazine, I was easy prey for San Francisco's moody stylishness.

I got a job as a cocktail waitress at a velvety hotel lounge, around the corner from some or other filming location of *The Maltese Falcon*, where I balanced silver trays overhead and played the role of wry and mysterious bon vivant. The lounge hired only girls with a certain look, and this heady knowledge carried me off to a place of ego from which there was no easy return. I began to drink Fernet Branca, Champagne, pricy tequila, and aperitifs and digestifs that I'd only ever seen people drink in old movies. I was twenty-four and insufferable. While I see this headiness now as an optimism reserved for the young, I see it also as a kind of privilege, for unconsciousness is a privilege.

Part of the headiness also came from the belief that nothing was real or permanent, that everything could be undone or redone or begun again. While traveling in pretty packs with my coworkers from bar to bar after work or flying off to Vegas with them because someone knew someone who knew someone who would comp our whole weekend, I knew I didn't belong to this world. Perhaps our entrée was just a collapsed time wave, and none of us belonged. Whatever stardust or magic propelled me then, I still remember these years both fondly and sheepishly, as a time when I fell through a portal to a place seemingly without consequences.

It feels like days have passed, but I realize it's more like an hour or two as I catch a glimpse of the outside world when the sally port doors rise to let in a police van of what the more seasoned women call "new fish." The light looks pre-dawn, blue limning the black edges of night. We're still waiting for the county bus, this motley assemblage of women, and we are growing antsy and cold, the air conditioner unit blasting like a jet engine. At my end of the table, there's a white office-type a few years older than I, who looks at me sympathetically; she has dishwater hair and wears a cardigan twinset. There's the blonde barfly in her early twenties who wears heavy maroon lip liner and pale gloss like the Puerto Ricans I knew in high school.

There's Big Bird, and there's me—barefoot, blood seeping through the thighs of my jeans, with a stretchy brown dress pulled over them to the knees in a way that seemed cute when I got ready for work earlier, but which now seems ridiculous, itself a cause for arrest.

In memory, the other inmates are a blur of light-skinned and dark-skinned faces, mostly Black or Brown. I want to say the other white women made an impression on me because we looked so out of place by comparison, because I felt conspicuously white, my skin on fire with its whiteness. I want to say that I wasn't drawn to them for kinship, yet it troubles me now why I should remember the white ones more clearly. But memory has its own story to tell, and this is in part the story of the beginning of my education, my other education.

I run through a panicked inventory of what I remember from earlier in the night: I crashed my Jeep. Icrashed-myJeepohfuckIcrashedmyJeep. Don't remember how I got to the pulsating intersection about a mile down the feeder road from the Tasting Room where I work.

I came to while standing barefoot on one leg in Yia Yia Mary's Greek Kitchen parking lot. A full-bloom accident scene—multiple crashed cars, at least three cruisers, lights swinging, the caterwauling crackle of radios breaking in and out, and voices bouncing all around me. A DWI task-force SUV was parked while black-clad officers shone their flashlights all around the Jeep. The traffic backed up in a smear of headlights down San Felipe Street. My face felt hot. I must have been drinking at work, as usual (maybe corked wine from the mug I have hidden in the work kitchen?). I must have left before the end of my shift.

Next, I was in the rear of the cruiser, my arms pressed together and hands clenched in a fist behind my back, playing a version of the old daisy game. *I knew. I didn't know. I knew.* Later, the arrest report and the statutory warning, which is made upon refusal of an alcohol breath test, would fill in other details, including that four cars were involved. It was a "Major Auto—A-A-A-A," which occurred at 10:50 p.m. The first three officers were dispatched at 11:05. Not long after arriving on the scene, they asked for a DWI task force, who arrived and performed a field sobriety test. Parts of this I remember (for example, my jeans rolled up like Huck Finn). At some point, it is also noted, an off-duty officer, one identified only as T. Ha "made the scene." The crash occurred at 1800 West Loop South and San Felipe, the weather conditions were clear with some clouds, and the roadway was dry. I was arrested at 11:57 p.m.

Sitting in the cruiser, I knew very little, other than that it was bad, the worst reckoning yet. Too much to hold in my body at once. I felt like one of those Whack-a-mole arcade games. As soon as I had stuffed down one unknowable truth, ghoulish and taunting, another leaped from its hole. All of what I worked so hard to contain around my drinking—its central ugliness, the lies and self-feints, the clanging empties and cigarette burns, the swallowed pills and stomach pumpings—sprang up around me.

In one depression of the gas pedal (Had I pressed it down hard, to the floor, and held my breath? Hadn't I?), every single thread came undone. My private mess was rendered public, splayed out at the intersection of San Felipe and the West Loop. This time I had made victims and carnage. And if the people in these other cars, three other cars containing an as yet unknown number of people, were victims, what did that make me?

As Officer S.W. Pierce wrote on a clipboard from the front seat, I put my knees up on the Plexiglas partition and slumped back in my seat, letting my head fall upon the window. The lights went around all helter-skelter, orbs of blue and white lurching at my eyes and head, then circling away and lurching again. I didn't cry, not then. I didn't try, but I knew I couldn't have opened the door from the inside.

I raised my head and asked the question that made it heavy. How were the other people in the accident? He didn't respond at first.

"Are they okay?" I asked.

"Not really," he said. "That lady is going to the hospital."

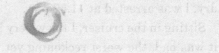

There were years that followed my initial and relative innocence in San Francisco when drinking was no longer fun, but it was habit. While my old friends moved on, I stayed at the bars, where I made new friends every night, or afternoon, or whenever. And when I wore out those places, I moved.

The "geography cure," I would learn later, was a popular remedy among drunks as it often pre-empted the falling hammer of consequence. And here again, I thought I had been unique—romantic, special, coursing with wanderlust and a keen appetite for the sensual world. The geography cure allowed you to outrun loss, leave before wearing out your welcome, start fresh, have a do-over. From age twenty-one to twenty-eight, I bopped from New England to North Carolina and back to New England and to San Francisco and back to New England before Houston at nearly thirty. This was how I had ended up here, with my brother, and our sad non-plan.

"I have to stop," I think, but more as a question, and this truth yanks me from my inventory. Some women down the table trade arrest stories with seasoned bravado. One in particular, a white, weathered old bird with fanned, feathered hair, conjures Aileen Wuornos. Still finishing the trays she's asked for and piled up around her, she shows more interest in my powdered eggs than in my personal drama. I pass her the eggs but keep the little hunk of cornbread I've been picking at for hours. Most of my fellow inmates arrived here this morning by way of drug charges, public intoxications, or prostitution. It occurs to me this would all be surreal if it wasn't actually happening.

I am unable to summon what my friend Ellen calls a writer's critical distance, a phenomenon of observation that affords one an aisle seat in life. Surrealism, irony; these rhetorical lenses will prove to be past-life luxuries, skins of a former self. Tonight, I am scrubbed down to my ugly core. The acuity runs too high: that lady howling coyote-like, and one over there trying to take a dump in the toilet while talking on the pay phone. One woman talks about having been "shanked up in county," and I have the presence of mind not to ask her what this means. I may be green, but I'm also at least half-New Englander, which means that stoicism was part of my early childhood training.

I've been here a few hours by the time I notice a list of phone numbers taped to the glass wall that stands between me and freedom. I've already tried my brother from the one sticky payphone, to no avail. As it turns out, mobile numbers cannot be dialed collect. I realize that I don't know many numbers by heart anymore. Plus, the characters I know these days are good only as drinking buddies; they aren't the types with connected cell service much less home telephones, much less the ability to make bail.

The two home numbers I can remember, in fact, are my own childhood phone number and my best friend's old number. Strangers live in our old houses now at 5 and 7 Carlene Drive, respectively, in Nashua, New Hampshire, but for a moment, I imagine myself dialing home. My dad answers from our little fiberboard kitchen; he's angry, and he makes the sucking fish face that he wears when he's mad, but then he comes to pick me up, and I know that he will fix everything.

After trying a few numbers from the list, I get through to one of the bail bonds offices, and a nice man takes down my information and promises to call the numbers I give him: my brother and my mother, in that order. While the bondsman has me on hold, I mouth-whisper a few inadequate prayers. *Please. Please. Please. Oh god, please be okay. Please tell me no one else is hurt.* I can't form the word "dead," not with my mouth nor in my mind.

Later, I'd find out that the bondsman got through to my brother sometime during the middle of the night. Josh thanked the bondsman but said he wanted to use another guy, his guy. My brother is a loveable hustler, so it didn't surprise me to learn that he had used his petty marijuana arrest from a few months before to develop a "relationship" with this other bondsman. Of course Josh knew this guy's personal cell number, this Rodney Tompkins, owner of Am-Mex Bail Bonds. Of course Rodney would bond me out that night without payment up front. He allowed us to bring by the money the following morning or once I got out of jail.

After making the call, I look for Big Bird. She's moved into one of the adjoining cells with bunks, and she waves me over. "Get a top one," she says. "No one will fuss with you up top." I climb into the bunk opposite hers.

"You think this is bad, County a dog pound," Big Bird tells me. "I just know I'm fixin' a be transferred over any minute. Ain't no one gonna bond me out. I bet you got people, you look like you got people." I nod. *I have people.* I had always had people.

When I didn't make the crappy B-team basketball cheerleading squad in eighth grade, I called Dad and gurgled my naked rejection into a pay phone by the school's loading dock. A few minutes later, his tan Datsun appeared, and I began to sob. "Get in," Dad said, and then he instinctively took the long way around the parking lot, avoiding the gymnasium entrance and ball fields, until we had made a clean getaway.

On a trip many years later, when an Italian waiter put his mouth on me in an apartment swirling with children's toys and my protestations, I used another pay phone. Dad said go to the embassy. He said the Marines will be there by the entrance. They will take care of you. You will be okay. *You have people.*

After another hour or so, a small group of us is herded out and led into a tiny office where we have to sit until we are called up to give our information to a lady through a grated window—full name, nickname, aliases, where we stay at, height, weight, race, eye color, birthplace, occupation, tattoos, mental illness, prescriptions, priors, medical conditions, and whether or not we are wearing our real hair.

"Chicago," the lady exclaims. "You a long way from home."

"Well, see, I live here now; I only lived there when I was a baby," I say, anxious to engage.

"Occupation?" she barks, without raising her eyes.

"Bar Manager." I leave off wine, as it now seems pretentious, ridiculous.

"Tattoos?"

"Yes." We are in a nice rhythm now.

"Well?" she asks, looking at me impatiently. "What are they?"

"Oh, yes, okay. Well, there's a little star on my hip and ..."

"Color?"

"Huh?"

"Colored or black?" she demands, annunciating slowly, and lifting her head as if in great labor, to look at me.

"Oh, black."

"Yes?"

"And the other is like this drawing I did of a lady with her head down and a waxing moon coming up over her shoulder."

Another wearied expression, this one just slightly bemused. "Say what?"

"It looks like a dolphin, you can just put down dolphin," I tell her, remembering the time Dad first saw it poking out of the top of my bikini when I was home from college. "A dolphin on your arse," he had observed, never mentioning it again.

"Well, now I have to see this," she says, motioning for me to stand up.

I stand up, face away from her, and hoist my dress to my waistband. I unbutton my jeans, aware that all the other women are eyeing me. I hook my thumbs into my jeans and panties, pull them both halfway down my butt, and let her take a look.

"Well, I don't know what that is," she says and calls over another officer. I hear them talking behind me.

"Whatcha call that? I have here dolphin."

The other lady agrees that dolphin is close enough, and I am allowed to sit back down. The Q and A goes on for a few more minutes before I am called out of the little room by another officer who pokes in her head and hollers.

"02150152!"

I check my number on my paperwork, like this is a game of BINGO.

"Yes, that's me."

"Well, come on, then," she says. My heart crashes in my chest and ears.

"Where are we going?" I ask her when we get into the hallway.

"You bonded out," she says, "you goin' home." I hear HOME. A delicious place of warm socks, hot food, hot tears, a bed.

I am instructed to sit in the hallway while she goes into another office. I watch her through the glass as she hums to herself, typing on keys, then pulls out a little metal tray. She's singing now and wags her body side to side as she waits for the printer. She emerges with a little baggie and some forms.

"Here's your paperwork and your property," she says, handing me the loose contents of my purse and leading me down a long hallway to a door that looks like a submarine hatch. She pops it open and holds the door for me to walk through. I am blasted by sun and heat.

"Go home," she says. "And don't come back."

I give her a nod and see Josh leaning against the hood of his Corolla, smoking a cigarette. He cocks his head to the side, "Hey, sis."

I walk over and hug him, still humming that tune in my head. *I have people.*

12. HOW ABOUT THIS FOR META?

An interview with the author by essayist, editor, and Luminarts Foundation Fellow, Michael Fischer, about jail, jail narratives, tropes, and hopes.

Background, The State of Texas vs. Alexis Paige:

In 2005, in Houston, I caused a car accident while drunk and was arrested for the first time in my life, at twenty-nine years old. A woman in one of the other cars broke her leg (and turned out to be an even more privileged white person than me), so after an initial misdemeanor charge, I was re-charged with a felony and faced two to ten years in prison. My case took over two years to adjudicate—during which time I was under pre-trial supervision (correctional control for those under felony indictment—what's up, presumption of innocence?!) and during which time I got what I now like to call my education, my real education. Ultimately convicted of a lesser-included misdemeanor and sentenced to 121 days (#whiteprivilege #goodlawyer

#intergenerationalwealth #drivingwhilewhite #presumedinnocent). I served sixty days (2:1 or "good time" credit is standard in county jail sentences) in the Harris County Jail, the third largest in America—with well-documented and horrifying rates of inmate deaths, civil rights violations, guard-on-inmate assault—including sexual assault, and the subject of an internal investigation, multiple AG investigations, and an investigation by the DOJ civil rights dept. Like many Americans and like most white Americans, I actually knew very little about the system, so I set out to write about what I'd learned, especially about whiteness and unearned privileges.

Michael's Questions

MF: Even at the best of times, many writers find it nearly impossible to put pen to paper. Prison is not the best of times. While inside, were you able to carve out a healthy writing environment and practice? If so, how? If not, how did you still get your work done?

AP: I made notes—to remember little details like how to make hot rollers out of tampons—but I didn't really write. My time was so short, the plan was just to get through it and get back to life and work once I was out.

MF: Understandably, inmates often use some form of escapism to get themselves through the day, be it television, fantasy novels, etc. Of course, as writers, we're called to do the opposite: to always be present to and observant of the world around us. How did you balance those two things—the instinct to emotionally protect yourself versus the need to be open to your creativity and humanity?

AP: This is sort of the same answer as above. With such little time to get through, I didn't feel pressure to maintain a serious creative practice. Mostly I passed the time. I was a year sober to the day when I began my sentence, so keeping up on that work was important, but otherwise, I slept (man, did I learn to sleep in jail—can sleep ANYWHERE now); I waited for the paper to come around; I called my folks every day; I got a visit from my now-husband almost every day; I read the gossip mags a girlfriend sent; I read Michael Crichton's entire oeuvre; once a week I got off the pod and played volleyball; I watched Selena on television twenty times; I wrote letters; I learned how to play dominoes and played dominoes; I taught some of the other girls yoga and helped them write futile letters to judges; I learned how to "perm" Black hair (relaxers) and did a dozen perms; I answered questions about white people—like do you really all love Starbucks? *Yes, most of us, I think.* And how can you stand country music? *I can't.* I ate Saltine crackers; I did crosswords; I passed the time.

MF: Writers often find themselves working in genres that seem to demand a particular narrative trajectory. A so-called addiction memoir must contain x; a so-called war memoir must contain y. Prison writing seems to suffer from this particularly. Many readers and the contemporary literary world have certain expectations of what prison writing is "supposed" to look like and the progression it must make—from ignorance to enlightenment, from crime to redemption. How have you approached and perhaps subverted these expectations?

AP: At some point I realized I didn't want to write merely a personal story, nor did I want to write an *Orange Is the New Black* sort of story—with its skimpy analysis and problematic tropes about both race and the prison. I also didn't want to write a rape memoir or an addiction memoir—though both are part of my story. At the same time, having served just sixty days in jail doesn't exactly make me an expert on incarceration nor a spokesperson for women inmates. I'm trying to write a bigger story—I'm loath to say "universal" because that itself is a backwards assertion—but my experience of jail was not representative of most, nor of most women.

For example, being white was an insurance policy against being raped by one of the guards in jail. Guard-on-inmate sexual assault is a well-documented problem in the Harris County Jail, one that provoked in me an initial panic. A history of sexual assault had escalated my drinking, which had led to jail, so the prospect of being raped again made my chronic-PTSD kick in. But at some point, maybe a couple of weeks in, I realized I probably wouldn't be raped. And I wouldn't be raped because by looking at me you knew I had people. And this knowing was a kind of visceral awareness—smarter than my own conscious awareness—of how race operates in our society, and even more so inside.

In an interesting paradox, the way to tell this larger story, I believe, is to focus on my own toxic whiteness and my experience of becoming more aware of it and how it made being snagged by the system more tolerable (e.g., I also knew that I didn't ever have to go back to jail, not unless I really fucked up)—not in a navel-gazing way so much as an allegory for whiteness in America. I am trying to write about how the criminal justice system exposed me to an America I was before only abstractly aware of. I don't feel that I, personally, am working against too many expectations in terms of genre/form. *Orange* is the obvious one, of course, but that expectation feels, well, silly. The gatekeepers don't know what they don't know. As I read other jailhouse memoirs and more about race, I discovered that I also didn't want to write a redemption memoir. As an educated, middle-class white woman who had once done some print/commercial modeling for eyewear and catalogs, I am not looked at as the sort of person who needs redemption anyway (which is exactly part of the problem). Almost everyone presumes my innocence, to a laughable extreme. This is the kind of voyeurism I get: what was it like? I can't imagine *you* in jail, etc. It's toxic, sure, but it's not the same as the negative stereotyping and voyeurism that most formerly incarcerated people experience. Having been in jail [as a white person] makes me interesting, spicy. It makes most people unemployable. So part of my calculus on redemption is to call bullshit on that trope in general, but also more specifically, to champion a kind of anti-redemption. Why do I deserve redemption more than anyone else? I don't. And I actually was guilty. But what bothers me even more about redemption is the false premise that underlies the expectation—that people who have been to jail are bad, should be "penitent," need reform or redemption. That premise says that most of the 2.3 million people we have locked up and the 6.8 million under correctional control deserve to be there. Or are there because of personal wrongdoing—and not because of some political agenda or ... old-fashioned racism and social control. So, fuck redemption, man. None of us needs to be redeemed for being human. And plenty of people are locked up simply for being poor and/or the wrong color. They don't need redemption, the system does. America does.

MF: Writing programs and literary journals say they want a diversity of voices and perspectives. Based on your experience—with MFA programs, publishing, nonprofits, and the job market—how well do you feel literary organizations are doing in making a place for the formerly incarcerated and other underrepresented groups?

AP: Here too, I don't think I am working against the same barriers as most formerly-incarcerated writers. I'm well-published, I'm an editor at a respected nonfiction journal, and while I don't have tenure yet, I do have a kushy academic gig and more work than I know what to do with from other opportunities. I'm very well-represented. My job is to use my opportunities and privileges—and also to give up some of them—to cede some space, opportunities, and privileges—to make sure not that representation improves (this seems to me a token prize) but that power and opportunities and structures become truly more equal. No, I don't think the literary world is doing enough. And throwing scraps at BIPOC writers and other marginalized groups isn't going to do it. We [myself included] need to give up some power. Nothing will really change until that happens.

ACT THREE:
ONCE MORE UNTO THE BREACH—STILL BEGINNING, EVER BECOMING

13. DIGGING FOR MUD BUGS AND STORY BONES

ABOUT HALFWAY through Barbara Hurd's 2016 essay collection, *Listening to the Savage: River Notes and Half-Heard Melodies*, I find myself splayed across a granite boulder in the middle of the small river that runs through my backyard in rural Vermont. Obviously, I am listening for crayfish. An avid river watcher, I confess that until reading this beautiful, brilliant book, I had not considered the role of river listener, or river monitor as Hurd calls herself. She points out that monitor derives from the Latin *monere*, which means to warn or advise—even to remind or teach, according to my old Latin dictionary. From my back porch, I often eye the river's movements, its patterns, its shimmer and light; I watch for deer, wild turkeys, ospreys, foxes, bald eagles, and the occasional Great Blue Heron.

Recently, in the shallows near the yard, a few kids appeared, pants hiked up over their knees and buckets swinging from their elbows. "What are you guys looking for?" I hollered from the porch.

"Mudbugs," one called back, "ten so far."

At fourteen, I was a budding scientist who won a National Science Foundation scholarship to the University of New Hampshire's month-long Mathematics and Marine Science Program, but I'm a long way from fourteen, and content now to marvel at nature through my camera lens or binoculars. And yet, with stirring pathos, *Listening to the Savage* has called me back to the river; more urgently, the book has summoned me to listen, "to turn my ear, that lonely hunter, and put it closer to the ground."

Listening, Hurd suggests, goes beyond observation and places the listener within the world: "If, as the ancients say, careful seeing can deepen the world, then careful listening might draw it more nigh. The eyes, after all, can close at will; we can avert a glance, lower the gaze, look elsewhere. But the ears, those entrances high on our bodies, doubled, corniced, aimed in opposite directions, can do nothing but remain helplessly open." If *Listening to the Savage* is a call to listen—to reclaim a sense perhaps atrophied by a culture of distraction and ubiquity—it is more siren call than polemic, for the author implores herself, as much as the reader, to do the difficult work of fully inhabiting the world, the mind, and the body. In the essay, "Practicing," Hurd describes her efforts at such presence—whether monitoring the river or practicing the piano:

> *I'm trying to see what it's like, in other words, not just to practice, but* to have a practice. *I'd like to reach a point where the choice to sit at the piano or go for a walk is less and less a choice and more and more simply what I do. Progress is*

> *gratifying, of course: a permanent ban on drilling matters, and a decent piano performance might be fun. But until then spending a little time every day with music and wandering the watershed with an ear to the river might eventually become a habit, like something one wears, not so much a garment, but skin, part of the body. Habit then might deepen to* inhabit, *to dwell in a place, maybe even a life. I'd like that.*

Hurd's seeking is a kind of devotion to listen to the world as it is, not for harmony or for discord—but for both.

"Here's my prayer," she writes in "The Ear Is a Lonely Hunter," the book's rousing opening essay:

> *Help us to listen to the sounds—fragmented, atonal, melodic, diminished, augmented—of our own lives and of the myriad lives among us: cricket trill, beaver whack, birdsong, snake hiss, donkey bray. Give me the voiced morsels of this child [her granddaughter, Samantha] ('Meemi, sometimes I get dark messages from my eyes'), unconducted love songs begun in the cattailly edges of a pond and the bellowy burp of bullfrogs. For this is the grounding, the sounding, things as they are, for now and for now. Amen.*

At the end of the essay, Hurd explains how vision "is deepened by listening, especially if the ear has turned from any wishful music of the spheres and heard, as if for the first time, the whoosh of wind in the trees or the cry of a red-tailed hawk." It calls to mind Susan Sontag's entreaty in her essay, "Against Interpretation," in which she argues that the overproduction of art has blunted a kind of collective, cultural sensory awareness. Sontag writes, "What is important now is to recover our senses. We must learn to see more, to hear more, to feel more."

The essays in *Listening to the Savage* offer up rich explorations of literature, epistemology, love and family, science and place, and even of attentiveness itself. The meanderings of the author's mind—whether quibbling with Thoreau or poring over her father's letters from his seventeen-month internment in a German POW camp—often wend along those of the book's titular river, the Savage in Western Maryland. In prose that is stunning, searching, precise, querulous, and revelatory, Hurd demonstrates how attentiveness can be the writer's best instrument. Such is perhaps the larger hypothesis of the book, which calls upon the reader to listen deeply, whether for its own sake or that of art or the planet.

This was how I came to commune with the crayfish who seemed to be sunbathing on the rocks exposed by an unusually-parched riverbed this summer, as New England experienced one of the worst droughts in its history. *Listening to the Savage* prompted me to attune my hearing in much the same way that Annie Dillard's *Pilgrim at Tinker Creek* made me see the act of seeing itself. You know that old saw that goes something like fish can't see the water they swim in? I had no awareness of my own hearing, no clarity of sense, I realized, as I sat on the rock waiting for the crayfish to speak. I didn't know how to listen to crayfish, of course, so I meditated intensely for many minutes, pleading with my ears to work and with my auditory senses to tune into some deeper source. I could hear the river, the cows across the way, cars buzzing by, but no crayfish. Perhaps they were soundless creatures, like arthropodal mimes, I thought, climbing up the riverbank and back toward the house, but no, I had read about the clicking sound—had listened to a recording online of a stridulating crayfish clicking furiously around an underwater rock cave that made me imagine crustacean pinball. I had been bitten by a kind of mudbug fever, but more than that, I was mimicking the exquisite listening that Hurd performs in the book; I was seeking connection. I began to comb maps of the White River Watershed, looking for mile markers, like those that mark certain chapters in the book. If I found mile eleven, for example, of my own river, perhaps I might locate the heady vibrations of Hurd's prose: "Want to deepen your nostalgia? Imagine you're a river that believes in *once upon a place*." Possessed with an idea that the waters of my river might somehow mingle with Hurd's Savage, in some forgeable intersection, I began to trace the two rivers on separate maps. Alas, our rivers don't meet, at least not on the watershed maps. The Savage runs into the North Branch of the Potomac, then into the Potomac, then into Chesapeake Bay and the Atlantic Ocean, while the White River runs into the Connecticut, then into Long Island Sound and the Atlantic some three-hundred miles northeast. When I began looking at maps of ocean currents and the path of the Gulf Stream, I realized I had gone too far; I didn't need a map to tell me that I was connected to this book.

In essays that weave modes of lyricism, narrative, research, and social commentary, Hurd takes the reader on a sublime listening journey. Whether recording her granddaughter's quirky wisdom ("Some dreams you tell and some you don't"), or raindrops while channeling a spadefoot toad, or the dehiscence of fern annules when they "all start snapping like a legion of catapults," or the interior alert that called the author out of an early marriage, Barbara Hurd's voice sings. "I don't know why certain sounds—wind chimes on the back porch, loon calls, that big owl's silence—can open an ache in me," she writes. "I only know—at least for the moment—that today's steady hiss of snow on snow works like a psst in my ear, making the mundane both more mundane and less: *mundus*, after all, means *the world*." In the essay, "To Keep an Ear to the Ground," Hurd writes, "Sometimes when I put my ear to the ground, I make my own arbitrary rules: No listening for anything I might expect. No listening for anything that has a plan for me. No listening to anything that knows I'm listening. No pretending to listen to what bores me utterly." I realize that my efforts to listen to the basking crayfish were hampered by two things. First, I was pretending. Second, I should have been listening and watching, for if I had taken a closer look, I would have seen that the brittle, desiccated creatures were not sunbathing at all, but dead. Next time, I'll turn away from wishful music, put my ear to the ground, and listen for whatever the world brings. To hear things as they are, *I'd like that.*

14. LILACS IN THE DOOR YARD*

Common Purple Lilac: "A mass of medium-light purple blooms every year. A magnificent New England sight for nearly 400 years. When a nursery friend looked out John's living room window and thought he had some fancy new cultivar, he chuckled, 'Nope, just the good old common purple.' Never disappoints. Suckers freely, the best lilac for a spreading hedge. *Syringa vulgaris*" Description from the Fedco Seed Catalog

When lilacs last in the dooryard bloom'd,
And the great star early droop'd in the western sky in the night,
I mourn'd, and yet shall mourn with ever-returning spring.

Opening Stanza of "When Lilacs Last in the Dooryard Bloom'd," by Walt Whitman

"Can you believe I drive a friggin' Volvo?" I text one of my oldest friends. We trade shorthand code, the sort developed with those who have seen you through many decades and phases—the well-scrubbed-coed-ordering-amaretto-sours-without-irony phase; the hairy-armpits-

and-knockoff-Birkenstocks-with-wool-socks phase; the slaggy-handkerchief-halter-top-and-bumps-in-the-bathroom-with-the-drummer-or-was-it-the-bassist-from-Metallica phase; the can-you-believe-I'm-still-bartending phase; the can-you-believe-I'm-in-rehab-and/or-jail phase; and now this, the can-you-believe-I'm-driving-a-Volvo-and perimenopausal.

"You in a Volvo station wagon is the most ridiculous thing I've ever heard of," my friend fires back.

"You are *literally* the whitest you have ever been." I don't argue, nor could I. Now in my forties and out of the feigning street cred game, I seem by most external measures happy and stable—rooted even. I have something akin to that domestic dream which Zorba the Greek lamented in the 1964 film: "wife, children, house, everything, the full catastrophe." I have a devoted husband, an accountant who is also the town fire chief, a bric-a-brac of teaching and editing gigs that passes for a career, three mature lilac bushes, and 2.2 dogs. Keith and I joke that our three-year-old boxer, George, whose name is loosely derivative of Seinfeld's George Costanza, counts as 1.2 dogs, the extra two-tenths owing to his extra alpha-dog-bro-ness. But this exterior sketch isn't false, just thin. Anthropologists and other social scientists favor a "thick description" of human behavior, which explains not only the behavior itself but also its larger context. What I suppose they mean is that the human condition is a motherfucker.

Beyond our Fisher-Price town with its steepled square and mix of Colonial and Victorian storefronts winds the small river that hugs our country road. Between this river and road, farms nestle—some ramshackle, some picturesque—in the furry, coniferous hills of central Vermont. If you scrub past the rosy patina of Norman Rockwell Americana, you find ordinary America too, or perhaps 'Murrica, as some of my local students like to declare proudly: blue tarps and Gadsen flags, guns, black tar heroin, snowmobiles, high rates of domestic and sexual violence, and other assorted clichés of rural poverty and disease. Down this road a few miles sits the 1830s farmhouse that Keith and I bought the summer after my MFA, flanked on one side by hay fields and on the other by the not-so-mighty but lovely First Branch of the White River. Because we lived in Arizona when I was a child and swimming pools were ubiquitous, Mom plunked me in a toddler swim class at two, and I've been a water lover ever since. Given a chance to swim, especially in the wildness of an ocean, lake, or river, I will stay submerged for hours—until my skin prunes. Here, in the town of just over a thousand souls that we now call home, I watch and listen to the river daily from our back deck. If the weather is warm and the river high enough, I head down to the water for a dip or to sit on a giant granite boulder, deposited as glacial moraine during the last ice age, and marvel at my luck. Calling this place, any place, home does a number on my psyche, yet here, I am making peace with the full catastrophe. Something I can't yet name washes over me, or perhaps that something is finally washing away.

Nearly fifteen years earlier and six thousand miles from my apartment in San Francisco where I lived in my twenties, I sat nervously in a cold, stone office in the bowels of the stazione policia, on Via Zara in Florence, Italy. I was twenty-five, and on my first trip abroad. The night before, I shared dinner with friends on the Piazza Della Repubblica, fifteen minutes by foot from the police station. The night before, I wore an outfit I bought especially for the trip: tight red pedal pushers and tight red blouse, heeled sandals, and purple head scarf. We chatted gaily with our waiter, who joined us for Fernet Branca and Prosecco after his shift. He spoke little English, and I little Italian, but in broken Spanish and flirty eye contact, we managed well enough. My friends and I and the waiter walked over the Ponte Vecchio, but at some point while browsing the trinket shops and smoking cigarettes with our arms draped through the stone portholes over the Arno, he and I drifted from the group. At another point, I figured they'd gone back to our hotel, and he offered a "corto trayecto" on his moped. Still drunk and sun-baked from the day, intoxicated by the wafting lilac and street disinfectant, and dizzy from the ridges of terracotta rooflines undulating by, the ride exhilarated me in those first moments. But after twisting down more dusty lanes and bumping over cobblestones and emerging onto a faster, wider boulevard, my giddiness evaporated. I began to feel sick and to spin, adrift from my friends and our hotel and the center of town. He slowed the moped to a stop, hopped it onto a sidewalk in front of an apartment building, and with his strange, sweaty hand, the nice-seeming waiter led me up a flight of steps and into his small apartment.

We got here as soon as we could, my husband and I like to say—both in a literal and metaphorical sense—about our arrival in Vermont, about how we are late bloomers, about how long it's taken to arrive at some place we might call home. We came to Vermont in 2007, fleeing Houston, Texas, in a little hatchback packed with everything we owned. We drove past the Texas refineries and Louisiana swamps, then into the lush hills of Mississippi and Alabama, and on through the Smoky Mountains and Shenandoah Valley. When we reached the Maryland panhandle, I knew the Mason-Dixon Line was close, and once over that arbitrary boundary, my body flooded with relief, as if I had been safely extracted from behind enemy lines.

I say that we fled because at the time we felt that we had to get out of Texas if we wanted to make it. A few months before I met Keith, I got drunk and crashed my Jeep into three other cars at a major city intersection. Miraculously, and despite epic vehicle wreckage, no one was killed and only one person was hurt. After my initial arrest for drunk driving, I was charged with a felony that carried a two- to ten-year prison sentence, and the ensuing, protracted legal ordeal loomed over everything, including our budding romance. Dating tips don't cover how to handle the "I'm under felony indictment" conversation on the first date, but Keith stayed, even as life became a two-year blur of court hearings, AA meetings, endless chauffeuring and bus rides, sporadic paychecks from temp agencies that would overlook my circumstances and pre-trial supervision, and finally, a five-day felony trial. I was more fortunate than most who get devoured by the Harris County Criminal Court system, convicted ultimately of a misdemeanor and sentenced to just 121 days in the fearsome Harris County Jail. With good time, I served sixty.

My lawyer's early admonishment about the Texas criminal justice system proved prophetic: "You might beat the rap, but you won't beat the ride." While on the ride, Keith and I talked about "going home" once everything was over. Despite early years out West, I had spent much of my youth in New Hampshire, and on visits to New England Keith became enamored of the beauty, history, and landscape. He grew up in Texas, but as someone who is naturally taciturn, who loves flannel, snow, and early mornings, I suspect he was a New Englander in a past life. While in jail, and with a firm end date and real second chance in hand, we finally began to make plans in earnest. Even though it was considered contraband, I kept a photograph stuck to my bunk with the adhesive strips from a stamp book so that I could remember what waited for me on the outside. It was a picture of Keith and me, from the trip we took to Vermont for my thirtieth birthday, standing outside in an October snow flurry. Vermont had become our new starting line.

Why did I go with the waiter? This was the tortuous refrain that ran through my mind the morning after, as I sat in the police station. I didn't speak Italian, but I found a sympathetic translator from the American Consulate who escorted me to the station to help me file a report. Why did I go? I thought, as she mouthed the

Italian words for the images that stabbed into my mind as if from a knife. The words sounded cheerful when this nice lady spoke them in Italian, the words for *oral sex*, for *finger penetration*, for *erect penis*, for *without consent*, for *kick-start scooter*, for *Champagne headache*, for *swarthy waiter*, for *slim build*, for a *Calabrian driver's license*, for *his email address scrawled on a napkin*, for *No*, for a *partial apology in Spanish*, for a *cigarette afterward*, for a *walk over the only bridge in Florence to survive World War II*, for *permission to call my father*, for *the correct change in Liras*.

A movie about my twenties would begin happily. A young, quirky Ally Sheedy would star, Sofia Coppola would direct, and most of my boyfriends would be played by John Cusack. These early adult years weren't without bumbling and angst, but for the most part, I had my act together. I lived in my dream city, where I was on track to complete a master's program in creative writing. I had my own studio apartment on Russian Hill, a tight group of friends, and steady, lucrative work as a cocktail waitress, which helped me save up for my first European adventure. The itinerary dazzled me—Paris, Amsterdam, Switzerland, Italy, Provence, and finally, Spain—but I never made it past Florence. So despite the auspicious beginning of my fantasy movie, the film would end unhappily, would tumble perilously thereafter across the screen, in a non-linear montage of depression, substance abuse, and suicide attempts, or what one shrink euphemistically called "gestures." Not even the best film editor could suture these storylines. The jump cut was too rough.

This twist in my story has only recently, all these years later, begun to rise to a place from which I might access and write about it. It's the story of, and here's the problem ... my rape? Or, my sexual assault? The first term I associate, technically, with penile-vaginal penetration, and the latter with euphemism. None of what happened feels technical or easily categorized, and neither does it seem deserving of euphemism, a language akin to evasion. See how the words still confound me, how the taxonomy remains fraught? I suspect that when the writer becomes a statistic, the language has to be dealt with as much as the event. *Is rape what you want to call it?* my father said to me in those early days. Of course, he didn't mean harm. We don't learn how to talk about such things in our culture, least of all men, least of all middle-aged fathers whose daughters call from payphones halfway around the world to say, *Daddy, I've been raped.* While I understand his quibbling now as an effort to make the thing somehow lesser or more manageable, or perhaps as an effort to attach language to the nightmare that we all could then live with, those words damaged me. I felt misunderstood and silenced, as if I couldn't be trusted to name my own experience. Though legal language varies, RAINN, the Rape, Abuse & Incest National Network, defines rape as, "Penetration, no matter how slight, of the vagina or anus with any body part or object, or oral penetration by a sex organ of another person, without the consent of the victim." Even though, technically, my experience does fit the definition, the truth is that I remain ambivalent about whether to call what happened to me rape.

Not long after the incident, the translator stopped returning my emails. Over time, I got mail from the Italian court that I couldn't read. One letter came. Then maybe another. This timeline, too, is fuzzy, mired as these months were in heavy drinking and a growing dalliance with cocaine. When I returned from Italy, I holed up in my boyfriend Mike's nondescript apartment in the Outer Richmond, which in those years was still a working-class neighborhood on the northwestern corner of the peninsula. His apartment was closer to my university and far away from my friends who lived downtown. Its location conscribed a small, anonymous circle of the city in which I could limit my travel and social activity. I felt safe only in the darkness of his apartment and zipped into the anesthesia provided by the drinking. But the safety was an illusion, the alcohol and drugs provided only temporary relief, and if anything, they slickened the slippery in-roads of my mind. Previously closed-off territory opened up, as if in a nightmarish version of Chutes and Ladders, wherein I replayed every slutty thing I'd ever done and every unpleasant encounter.

Long buried before, I suddenly remembered another assault, dredged from the depths of my consciousness like a car hauled from a riverbed, mud-caked and slick with algae. I was seventeen that time, and in my first week of college at Rutgers University in central New Jersey. Late in that first week, a junior from my dorm, a fast-talking, animated guy from Jersey City, took an interest. Now, of course, I know I should have been wary of a guy whose opening line to my roommate and me was, "You'se freshmen?", but then I was charmed. His accent and swagger were so different from the Boston-Irish guys I grew up with, and he was not just some immature high school boy but a college student—a man. Within minutes he was showing me his Don Mattingly swing impression and inviting my roommate and me to his dorm room for movies later that night. We went, of course, and while my roommate made out with his roommate (another beefy guy from Jersey City) beneath the Under-the-Sea phantasmagoria created by a spinning lava lamp, he made a move on me. We kissed for a minute, but a hunger in his movements frightened me, and before long I demurred, asking him to "slow down." But he was somewhere else, his eyes glazed and fixed on the wall behind me. In fact, he sped up after I said that, as if further aroused, and then rolled on top of me.

"C'mon, baby," he grunted, grinding his erection into my thigh. I tried to push him off of me, but he wouldn't give.

"Please stop," I said shakily, looking over at my friend who seemed oblivious and tangled up with the roommate. I assumed happily so, but I have wondered since, what if she had been in trouble too? How could I know what I was seeing, having never been taught what to look for? He pulled up my shirt and took my breasts in his mouth, suckled hard and with his teeth, then cupped my crotch over my jeans, rubbing his thumb hard back and forth against the zipper, which is where I imagine that he imagined my clitoris was. Finally, I managed to wiggle free by shimmying up the bed and wriggling out from between his legs. I hopped off the bed, pulled down my shirt, grabbed my bag and shoes, and clutched them to my chest to hide my breasts, which were still loose from the bra that was now pulled around my shoulders like a sash. I hurried to the door with the man panting after me. "Don't leave," he begged. "I promise I'll be good. You're just so sexy, baby." But once I was in the threshold of the door, he turned off the charm like a switch, and snarled after me down the hallway, "Bitch." It's probably important to point out that Rutgers, a state school where most students' hometowns were no more than two hours away, was desolate on the weekends—an additional factor that made my roommate and me, two rubes from out of state, easy prey. As I rounded the corner to the freshman wing of the dorm I heard him holler the charming words that my roommate and I later turned into a kind of revenge refrain: "You can't just leave me hanging! You gotta jerk me off or sumtin'."

The Boyfriend worked long hours as an options trader, but I remember that one night he came home early with takeout. I couldn't tell you whether this happened six weeks or six months after the rape, nor whether it was meant as a gesture of kindness or normalcy or even as a gesture at all, but his early return with dinner was unusual. Without much comment, I took a plate heaped with fried rice and egg rolls and my tumbler of White Russian and plunked down on the floor in front of the television in the living room. I had gained maybe fifteen pounds since the assault, and while I was nowhere near fat, neither was I the lithe ingénue he began dating years before. We were on the outs anyway, so what he said to me then—while not untrue—didn't penetrate my new armor. I was fortified by then, had taken up residence in my own sad kingdom. Standing in the doorway, his arms crossed, and with a mix of tenderness and perhaps disgust, he said, "Where is my bright, beautiful girl? I don't recognize you anymore."

I smiled wryly, raised my cocktail as in a toasting gesture, and said, "That, my love, is exactly the point."

I spent less and less time at my own apartment, which now seemed a place belonging to another person and time, a "before" shot from the "before and after" portrait of my own life. Through a bartender friend, I had lucked into the cute, cheap, central rental. No one I knew paid $700 for a studio in the heart of the city, let alone one with a private garden patio that teemed with bougainvillea, lavender, rosemary, eucalyptus, and the Purple Chinese Houses that looked like ornate, amethyst bib necklaces. The elderly, house-bound woman who lived upstairs had cultivated the garden for decades, but since she could no longer enjoy it, the garden became my private Eden—an idyll rich with a bracing cologne of eucalyptus and herbs. But that was before. After, I preferred exile.

No one seemed to want to talk about the assault anyway, or no one knew what to say, but perhaps that characterization isn't fair—or even accurate. Memorably, someone did say something—just the right thing, in fact. In a hand-written note on delicate ivory stationary, Jenna, a motorcycle-riding, beer-drinking girlfriend originally from Down East Maine, wrote: "You are the purest little rosebud, just beginning to flower. Please don't let this stop your petals from opening to the sun. Remember, in the end it is harsh pruning and bull shit that makes the rosebush grow strong." Perhaps I convinced myself that it was easier for everyone else, when I meant that it was easier for me, to forget the whole thing. After all, it happened a continent away, in another language even. The more that time passed the fuzzier and more distant the details became. Occasionally I would pull out the Italian paperwork from a file box. Four documents summarize my sexual assault: a report made by my friends; an initial filing made by me at a mobile police unit; a complete report made to the Florence Police; and a notification I received from the court many months later, and which as far as I can make out, gave me twenty days to declare a domicile in Italy. I can read Spanish, and the languages are close, but the documents are still hard to decipher. I thought about getting someone to translate them for me over the years, but again it seemed easier to let it lie, to let the words, and therefore the event, remain a kind of secret or mystery that I kept even from myself. In a sense, then, I answered my father's rhetorical question about what to call it by default, be deciding not to call *it* anything, to put the whole thing in an unlabeled box, and bury it on some godforsaken alien continent inside me.

Why did I go? I hate that I still ask myself this. I know this what-if game leads only to self-blame and shame, but I play anyway because this is what sexual assault victims do. Perhaps I shouldn't have worn red, shouldn't have flirted, and shouldn't have asked where we could get some pot. But, it was my girlfriend's boyfriend who asked, and the waiter who said he had some in his apartment. He said his apartment was just around the corner, and we could ride over there on his moped. He seemed so nice, so harmless. I should never have gone, should have said "no" more forcefully, should have kicked his teeth in—*something*. But what magical thing would I have done? I play this game, as all victims do, because our culture trains us to blame ourselves. Instead of teaching boys and men not to rape, we teach girls and women the dubious art of avoiding rape, and yet when, inevitably, women are raped, they are abandoned, or worse, they are re-victimized by a legal system that reinforces its own bogus mythology. Every case becomes her word against his, despite empirical research that puts false reports as low as with any other violent crime. After mustering the courage to report these crimes in the first place, victims fight again to convince police, prosecutors, judges, and juries, when ultimately, ninety-seven percent of rapists receive no punishment at all (RAINN). The message is clear: victims must bear their own burdens. We must learn how to survive our own rapes.

Though many of the direct memories of my assault remain sealed in drums and buried like radioactive waste or time capsules under hard-pack, I am still not safe from them. Trauma interacts with memory in complex ways, so memories of certain events—flashes—appear to me as non-linear images and sensory details. I am not unique in this. In an article for *Time Magazine* (December 9, 2014) on the neurobiology of sexual assault, Drs. James Hopper and

David Lisak explain why rape and trauma survivors have fragmented and incomplete memories of their traumas:

> *In states of high stress, fear or terror like combat and sexual assault, the prefrontal cortex is impaired–sometimes even effectively shut down–by a surge of stress chemicals. Most of us have probably had the experience of being suddenly confronted by an emergency, one that demands some kind of clear thinking, and finding that precisely when we need our brain to work at its best, it seems to become bogged down and unresponsive. When the executive center of our brain goes offline, we are less able to willfully control what we pay attention to, less able to make sense of what we are experiencing, and therefore less able to recall our experience in an orderly way.*
>
> *Inevitably, at some point during a traumatic experience, fear kicks in. When it does, it is no longer the prefrontal cortex running the show, but the brain's fear circuitry—especially the amygdala. Once the fear circuitry takes over, it–not the prefrontal cortex—controls where attention goes. It could be the sound of incoming mortars or the cold facial expression of a predatory rapist or the grip of his hand on one's neck. Or, the fear circuitry can direct attention away from the horrible sensations of sexual assault by focusing attention on otherwise meaningless details. Either way, what gets attention tends to be fragmentary sensations, not the many*

> *different elements of the unfolding assault. And what gets attention is what is most likely to get encoded into memory. ("Why Rape")*

Not only are the memories fragmented, but because again of the nature of trauma, and despite my best efforts to neutralize them, the memories intrude in on my thoughts without warning. One moment I am sitting by my river at home, and the next I am back in Florence, holding my friend Bernadette's hand, then tap-dancing on cobblestone, eating pasta, on the back of a moped. Suddenly, the man's fingers are inside me. His tongue inside me. I am crying. His penis is in my mouth; is that right? I am crying in his kitchen, asking for a ride to the hotel. Then I am back with my friends, outside the hotel, in relative safety under some streetlights. Bernadette and I are having a cigarette, and I am racing to tell her before the man gets back on his moped. As I tell her the story, the man is apologizing, inexplicably, to Bernadette's boyfriend. *Where's my apology?* I want to scream.

I am still waiting.

Perhaps because I am just now unearthing my sexual assault, it doesn't occur to me until all these years later, when my husband points it out, that this game, as I've always thought of the obsessive event replay, is a textbook hallmark of Post-Traumatic Stress Disorder. One morning not long after moving into the house, we are out on our deck, drinking coffee and admiring the view of surrounding mountains, meadows, and the river. The lilacs, which light up with pleasure from the same brain circuitry that alights with fear—the amygdala—are still in bloom, and the river is running high. Listening to the rush of the water, I tell Keith about the compulsion I have to replay the night over and over. "You know what that is, right?" he asks. I shake my head, even as I guess that I do. "It's PTSD," he says. I do it with the car accident, too, another trauma. I'd always assumed because in both instances I was drunk, that the replay was more about getting the narrative straight, trying to fill in certain holes. Is the inability to fill in the holes, trauma, alcohol, memory, or all the above? I run the replays automatically, absently, while drifting off to sleep or walking the dogs or washing the dishes. Each starts as a kind of mental video game, with Player One (me) flashing on the screen, and then we're off. Either we're running the crash scenario in Houston or we're running the moped scenario in Florence, each a sort of gauntlet where I imagine I can get points if I can lock certain features in place. Perhaps I can grab a new street name, a new weapon, or a new clue. Invariably, of course, the features of the game blur. So too with the features of memory, which escape me, bringing me once again upon the giant sinkholes that open up and swallow time, matter, memory, me.

"Lex," Keith says, waving his hand in front of my face the way we do to inquire if the other person is paying attention. And with that I come to, having been belched from the beast of my past, returning to our morning in progress.

"I don't know what's worse," I say. "The sudden jerks into the past, or the fact that I can never seem to stay in the present." I try then to settle into my chair, my body, my breath.

"Be where your hands are," my yoga teacher says. I study my hands, my oversized mug, and the lilacs in the yard, so purple they are almost blue. With their heart-shaped leaves and from the way they cluster into crown-like bunches, they remind me of the swim bonnets worn by the elderly women at my fitness center. But the fragrance is so unique that it reminds me of nothing but itself.

High on adrenaline and instinct and a life-long good sense of direction, the morning after my assault, I led the officers back to the man's apartment, which was not just around the corner as the man had suggested, but rather, some four-plus back-switching miles from the piazza. Since I had the napkin with his name and email address, the officers matched it with one of the occupants listed in their records. "Ben Fatto!" one of the officers shouted and pumped his fist from the front seat of the little police car.

"It means good job," the translator said.

"I know," I said. While still parked in front of the apartment, the officer craned around to face me in the back seat. He began talking intently, passionately, and looking back and forth between the translator and me. "He says he's very sorry this happened to you, and this is good evidence, but these things are hard to prosecute," she said. I nodded and thanked him. He turned forward as if to drive off but twirled back again, this time addressing mainly the translator. I made out the last word, *comune,* common. I looked at the translator, and she shook her head.

"C'mon, tell me," I said.

"There's no precise equivalent in English," she sighed. "It doesn't mean quite the same thing, but he says these things happen. They are common."

When I packed for my flight just hours later, I flattened the words on the police report in the bottom of my suitcase like a freighted souvenir, underneath the red pants and blouse and stacked heels I wore the night before. I realized then that my panties were gone, probably still in the man's apartment. Once on the plane and headed back to California, my seatmate asked if I was going home, and I nodded, then faltered. "Well, yes, I live there," I said, thinking home was not a word I understood anymore, not a place on any map.

The night we closed on our house, Keith and I stood in the back yard at dusk with our hands clasped. We had two dogs, a ten-year-old rescue pit-bull mix named Jazzy, and George, the Boxer tween we got a year after our first Boxer died. As a puppy, George, white- and fawn-colored with a comical black and brown eye patch of fur, was predictably mischievous, but it was Jazzy who—upon visiting the house for the first time that evening—had gotten so excited that she arched over in the entry way and took a massive dump. We were still giggling about it as we stood in our new yard, watching George zoom around the acre in obsessive circles, doing his "racetracks." The river was high and the lilacs in bloom, and the music from the water and the perfume from the flowers washed over us. "This is ours," Keith said, squeezing my hand a little harder.

"Yep," I said, squeezing back.

The common purple lilac, or *syringa vulgaris*, like those in the loamy northwest corner of our own yard, is a flowering woody plant in the olive family. Olives thrive in temperate, Mediterranean climates so unlike the harsh, snowy winters and humid summers of Vermont that it surprises me to learn this. I know it's greedy and provincial, but I've always associated lilacs with New England, which somehow made them mine. After all, the common purple lilac is the New Hampshire state flower, which I was forced to memorize in school, along with the state bird (purple finch), state fruit (pumpkin), state gem (smoky quartz), and state insect (the ladybug). But I do remember lilacs in Italy, whose fragrance stood out to me amid the other Florentine scents—amber, tobacco, lavender, cypress—as a kind of olfactory beacon of home. The family name, *syringa,* comes from the Greek word syrinx, or hollow tube, which refers to the plant's shoots and their large piths, while the species name, *vulgaris*, means common or usual. However ubiquitous lilacs may be, nothing about their loveliness seems common to me.

Later that night, while washing dishes and looking out the kitchen window that overlooks a side yard where the previous owners had a sizeable fenced-in garden, I tell Keith about everything I want to plant. I am excited, and the list grows absurd: star fruit, melons, Christmas trees, cucumbers, potatoes, peonies, roses, bleeding hearts, corn, lilies, bananas, chips and salsa trees, puppy seeds, and book awards. Keith laughs. I've never been a gardener, never planted anything other than pain, but in my fortieth year, I want to plant something, finally, that can thrive.

We'd been in the house six months when, and while unpacking the last of the boxes, I find a package marked "FRAGILE" in Keith's neat handwriting. I can't think of anything fragile we own—no valuables or heirlooms—but as I peel back the layers of plastic shopping bags used as wrapping, I see a box, about the size of a shoe box, which I recognize immediately as the urn containing the ashes of our first dog, Jimmy. A ninety-pound Boxer with a heart and personality to match his size, Jimmy came with us from Texas and lived here in Vermont until he was thirteen. Losing him was eased by the wonderful staff of our local vet office, who treated the loss as their own. We opted to have him cremated, and when we went to pick up the ashes, they were stored in a pine box with a handwritten card taped to the lid. The card, which had a raised, lumpy paper heart affixed to it, read, "Plant this in loving memory." The veterinary technician who emerged from the back to tell us how sorry she was explained that the heart adornment contained wildflower seeds that we could plant. At the time we lived in an apartment and decided to hang onto the card until we found a place of our own. I show Keith the card and read the instructions out loud: "Remove adornment from card, plant in your garden, and wildflowers will blossom year after year." I ask him if he remembers the garden I was talking about our first night in the house. I hold up the card and touch the little heart adornment and say, "We can start with this."

15. WRITING IS HARD, AND IT TAKES A LONG TIME

"A writer is someone for whom writing is more difficult than other people."
THOMAS MANN

A FEW SUMMERS ago, I sat in an MFA workshop in an upstairs room of the old stone mansion on the coast of Maine where my MFA residencies were once held. From the outside and on that rocky coast, the old stone mansion perched on the edge so precariously it might have been romantic, what with the old house creaking under the collective creative labor of 100-plus eager writers, the warm, briny air washing into the room, and the singular light dappling Casco Bay, but I felt the sort of lassitude one sometimes feels when one is sweaty and covered in mosquito bites.

It was the middle of a heat wave, the middle of the residency, my inflammatory bowel disease was acting up, someone from my earlier workshop said that I wrote like a "butler" (meaning fancy?), and by then, I had heard "show, don't tell" 237 times. Not all the calls for writing in scene were directed at me, but 237 is one more than the allowable number of times the maxim can be repeated before you are permitted a psychic break. The afternoon workshop was better, but I was already cooked, and I imagined myself tearing my manuscript up into little strips, then folding the strips into my mouth like taffy, chewing, swallowing. Perhaps once I had everyone's attention, I would strip down to my cotton underpants and jump out the window and into the bay, shouting show, don't tell as I crawled arm over head over arm out into the Atlantic.

Breaking into my panic-fantasy, the super-smart novelist and memoirist, Susan Conley, declared, "Writing is hard, and it takes a long time." She said it off-handedly, but a hush clapped over the room, the way a hush is wont to do in the presence of wisdom. It was a mantra moment, a thank-the-universe moment, a hell-yeah-it's-hard moment. It was strangely freeing because sometimes I feel there's a conspiracy among writers to pretend it's easier than it is or that it doesn't take freaking forever. It took me ten years to write an essay the internet gobbled up in one week. I've been working on my first book (which will end up being my third book if I ever finish it) for eight years, and I worry it will never be good enough, will never be finished. It took me almost twenty years to become a good writer. If I'm lucky, it will take me another twenty to be great. So, say it with me, writers: WRITING IS HARD, AND IT TAKES A LONG TIME.

Knowing this and being aware of my own tendency for puritanical shame, I try to do my best to work hard when I can and to ultimately trust in the long game. Writing is a lifelong pursuit, not a month-long sprint, not a New Year's resolution, and not a zero-sum game. And yet, regardless of your efforts to control and tame the writing process or make it tidy, the process will get messy; writing is thinking, and thinking is messy. So do your best to come up with a process or system that works, but also know that writing is hard. And it takes a long time.

My writing advice, on the one hand, is to be wary of advice. To be wary of the magic formula, that if followed to the letter, means you are a real writer. On the other hand, like most artists, I am interested in others' processes; I am interested in what their days look like. Still, if I force emulation of some imagined perfect schedule, one that dictates meditative walks, or morning hours only, or some other constraint, I might sabotage my own. I might fail to see that my own, probably messier, sporadic approach, might be the one that works for me. There have been months or years in which I've kept faithfully to a schedule—bounded out of bed at a predetermined hour and written a prescribed number of words or for a prescribed number of hours. But life happens, and making incremental progress is sometimes the best I can do.

A regular practice is important, yes, but I will stop short of proclaiming that a daily practice is an absolute requirement. During my days some years ago, as a full-time teacher and MFA student, I fit in writing where I could. These days, as a full-time teacher and once-upon-a-time writer, I still fit it in where I can. On some days I don't write at all, and on others I am consumed by a project or a piece, and I might dip into the well for twelve hours straight.

Ultimately there's no way around putting in the time, digging in.

Some Advice Anyway:

- Lower your standards on drafts—play around, make mistakes, make a mess. Sometimes the purpose of a draft is to produce one clear idea or sentence. You may have needed three pages of runway to take off, but that's okay. You can cut the runway now and just keep the lift.
- Expect many drafts: the essay in Chapter 10 took ten years and probably—no exaggeration—at least twenty drafts. (And guess what? I'm still tinkering with it, even after the essay was published, nominated for a Pushcart Prize, and named a Notable in the 2016 *Best American Essays* series.)
- Don't let the perfect be the enemy of the good enough or of the completed task. Sometimes work needs time to incubate and may not be finished for years. Other work might be imperfect, but it needs finishing so you can move on to another project. Not everything you write must be an opus.
- Slow down: it takes time to develop a voice; to have interesting and complex experiences; to develop skills, techniques, and craft.
- Set attainable goals: writing skill takes time, practice, development, and more practice—just like any other skill. Be optimistic but realistic about your short-term goals (to fight through whatever frustration I encounter and complete this essay) and your long-term goals (to write a book).

- Do you. Don't compare yourself to other writers. (This one is difficult to practice, and the paradox, of course, is that some comparison can be useful.) But too much comparison of success or talent can be toxic and paralyzing. Your goal is to find the idiosyncratic you-ness that makes your writing come alive, to become the best writer that you can.
- Learn from your mistakes: take time to assess your own patterns of errors or weaknesses, and learn how to fix them or improve, and do better next time. Working with other writers, mentors, editors, and teachers/speakers can accelerate the process of assessing and improving your skills.
- Work in concentrated bursts: studies show that people are more effective if they work for discrete windows of time. So set a timer for twenty-five minutes and see how many pages you can churn out.
- Fight your tendencies in small ways. For example, if you are a procrastinator, rather than spending an hour rationalizing the wisdom of this approach, sit down and write a rough draft now—only a rough draft. See if that doesn't change the process going forward.
- Ask for help. Ask for help. Ask for help. Writers waste so much time playing hero. *I must figure this out alone!* But there's almost always someone available to help—a friend or colleague, a mentor, a beta reader, a community writing group—who can help you think about the problem in a way that you hadn't thought of and who wants to help you.

- Have a sense of humor and get to work. Did you wait until the last minute yet again? Go ahead and laugh at the absurdity of writing in the wee hours with only the glow of your laptop for light. Then put on your lucky hat and get to work.
- You won't beat the chair. All writers must do it eventually. To produce a piece of writing, they have to get in the chair and they have to write. Scientists are currently testing workarounds, but early results aren't promising. Now, we know of no better writing method than getting in the chair and writing. So, you may as well sit down early and often now while you still have time.
- And the chair gives not one single fuck about your feelings, so Walter Mosely is 100% right when he says in his Master Class trailer, "Throw all that fear out the window: it doesn't matter. Because it doesn't."
- Take a break.
- Rekindle your interest, find your own plot again, put down the thing that makes you stuck, and try something that isn't writing.
- When you feel your interest returning, do something writerly that is not ALL about you:
    - Find a writing buddy, go on a trip or retreat
    - Pitch a panel for a conference
    - Co-write an essay
    - Review some books
    - Interview some writers

16. TRAVELING COMPANIONS & FLYING PINBALL MACHINES: HOW TO LAUNCH AND LAND YOUR FLASH CNF, BY ALEXIS PAIGE AND PENNY GUISINGER

From the Flight Deck

[AIRPLANE PUBLIC ADDRESS SYSTEM ENGAGES] "Welcome from the flight* deck: Captain Penny Guisinger here in the cockpit with First Officer Alexis Paige. We're expecting a bumpy ride over the Essay Heartland, folks, due to weather from a high-pressure limbic system in the area, and strong headwinds out of the slipstream. Throughout the flight, we invite you to follow along by googling the essays visible from the port side of the aircraft. Sit back, relax, and thank you for riding the nonlinear skyways of Amygdala Air. We're next in line for departure, so I'm going to hand the stick off now to Alexis Paige who will guide us through take-off."

Your Airplane Safety Card

When working in the short form, as with flash creative nonfiction, the writer must be aware of certain limitations that don't exist for longer essays or memoir. Flash essayists must be more mindful of constraints of airspeed, fuel capacity, and range. While jumbo jets can trace slow, long arcs in the sky, can climb high on a steady heading, and can cross oceans with plenty of time for snacks and naps and movies, a smaller vessel is designed for quick hops, tighter arcs, lower altitudes, and few, if any, snacks. Put simply, flash pieces don't have the same specs as longer essays, which is why you can't bring as much baggage. Space is a premium. Choose carefully when you're packing. Bring fewer pairs of shoes. Fewer modifiers. Fewer plot points. You can still explore a big area, but you must craft your flight plan more carefully.

Takeoff: Getting the Essay into the Air

From six-year-old aspiring Space Camper to tween wannabe test pilot to twenty-two-year-old aerophobe to now middle-aged aerophile, I've always had a fraught, obsessive relationship with flying. You wouldn't know this to look at me or my CV, but you would from my television diet, which is heavy on programs like *Air Disasters* and *Terror in the Skies*, or from my internet history, which includes a bookmark to the *Turbulence Forecast* website, or from web searches like the following, done while watching Denzel Washington's utterly commanding performance in the 2012 movie, *Flight*:

- "Aviation scene in *Flight* realistic?"
- "Inverted flight and laws of physics"
- "If anyone could fly inverted, it would be Denzel, right? RIGHT?"

While inverted flight is not unprecedented, nor theoretically impossible, such maneuvering of a commercial jet is, at best (according to my Google "research"), unheard of. So what does any of this have to do with the craft of flash nonfiction? Dig if you will, dear reader, an aviation analogy that I picked up decades ago during one indelible take-off out of Boston's Logan Airport. It was a sticky summer day back East, with black anvils of storm clouds marching across the sky, and I sat slick with sweat and panic in the back row of some godforsaken DC-10—a jetliner so doomed even the cowboy pilots of the 1970s called it the "Death Cruiser." With an unintelligible chirp from the cockpit, the jet rocketed down the runway, lurched steeply from the quilted earth, and with the g-forces still pressing me into my seat, I swiveled to my seatmate, as one does—wide-eyed, mouth slack—for confirmation that we were all about to die. Slim and distinguished, with a silver toothbrush mustache and ramrod posture, my seatmate turned out to be more than just a convincing aviator from central casting. In fact, he was a commercial airline pilot (a real one) who just so happened to be deadheading to San Francisco. "Navy pilot," he grinned, gesturing toward the cockpit—confident, unequivocal. In the Navy, the man explained, pilots must take off and land "on a dime." I took this to mean from their aircraft carrier training, but he didn't elaborate, and I never bothered to verify the claim. He telegraphed so much credibility, the metaphor was too good *not* to be true, and anyway, who was I to defy the immutable laws of a possibly apocryphal flying primer and oversimplified secondhand physics?

V-1

My favorite keywords of take-off lexicon are V-1 and Rotate. V-1 (V, for velocity) is the speed beyond which takeoff cannot be aborted; it's the literal point of no return, the moment just before lift off. Vr, or rotate, is the speed at which the pilot pulls back on the yoke to pitch up the nose, after which the plane leaves the ground. I love this moment of suspension in flight, and I love it in flash, too, that inflection point when the writer achieves lift. Since the stakes are cranked-up in a short piece, you can't afford to idle or lollygag or taxi aimlessly. You've got to get in the air fast, like a Navy pilot.

It seems counterintuitive that a piece should achieve such lift with an unwieldy opening run-on sentence, not to mention a fairytale convention, but as Brian Doyle's 1998 essay, "Two on Two," from *Creative Nonfiction* shows, what works, well, works. And this opening works:

> *Once upon a time, a long time ago, I rambled through thickets of brawny power forwards and quicksilver cocksure guards and rooted ancient centers, trying to slide smoothly to the hoop, trying to find space in the crowd to get off my shot, trying to maneuver at high speed with*

> *the ball around corners and hips and sudden angry elbows, the elbows of twenty years of men in grade school high school college the park the playground the men's league the noon league the summer league, men as high as the seven-foot center I met violently during a summer league game, men as able as the college and professional players I was hammered by in playgrounds, men as fierce as the fellow who once took off his sweats and laid his shot-gun down by his cap before he trotted onto the court.*

Doyle's tumbling syntax, combined with a pile-up of outsized modifiers and dizzying imagery, mimics the freewheeling energy of a basketball court while also thrusting the piece forward with undeniable velocity. Narrative control is further heightened by the contrast of understatement in the next paragraph: "I got hurt, everyone does eventually; I got hurt enough to quit; back pains then back surgery then more surgeries; it was quit or walk, now I walk." The piece then eases out of the narrator's youth, shifting into a deeper, longer view of life and time: "The game receded, fell away, a part of me sliding into the dark like a rocket stage no longer part of the mission. Now I am married and here come my children: ..." I won't give away too much of what comes after this colon, except to say that it's another run-on paragraph, this one more dazzling and improbable than the first. (Spoiler: it works.)

Daisy Hernandez's 2017 essay, "Wings," from *Brevity*, takes another approach syntactically, but as with "Two on Two," the opening lines launch the piece with irresistible force and momentum. Both essays manage plenty of heft, too, as much with what remains off the page as on. The introduction does triple duty by placing the piece in the history of El Salvador's civil war, introducing the main character, and queuing up the poetry to come. The opening paragraph forms the leading edge of a wave that builds and builds throughout the first half of the piece:

> *It is the early eighties, the start of the civil war in El Salvador, and Maira is a child of the raindrops that come early in the summer. Thousands of raindrops. Maybe millions. Las lluvias. Desperate raindrops that smash into the mountains and the treetops, prod the soil and also the pebbles and flores, the earth forced into a river moving downward.*

With the gathering force of allegory and a firm command of tone, Hernandez does everything that longer essays do, and more, but with so many fewer words. Essays that successfully navigate this tricky equation capture the magic of flash. As Dinty W. Moore notes in a 2012 *River Teeth* interview with Jenny Patton, "The imperatives are the same, but everything is dialed up in a shorter piece."

For a final take-off example, consider Jericho Parms's 2016 *Brevity* essay, "Night." It gets into the air with a narrator hanging curtains in her new house "during a winter that just wouldn't quit," then loops back in time to her freshman dorm room, and then back again to the curtains, back to the dorm, back to the house, and so on. Along the way, the piece scales everything from geology to the galaxy to "a boy I knew in college who came to my dorm room one afternoon—a mass-market copy of Elie Wiesel's *Night* in the palm of his hand—to read for his sociology class." Next, Parms loops in Buchenwald and deft concrete imagery—linen curtains, charcoal on paper, a paper lantern made of mulberry and bamboo—to muse about, not only the origins of science, art, and religion, but also the collective human impulse to cloister and shelter and how we do or do not ever know anyone or anything. Have I mentioned that Parms does all of this in under 750 words? I say again, magic.

Cruising Altitude: In-flight Menu

Once your essay has achieved flight, you have to keep your passengers, er ... readers feeling safe and well cared for. Whereas on a transatlantic flight you might get a full meal, on a hop from LaGuardia to Dulles, you'll get four or five Goldfish crackers in a bag so tiny it's invisible to the naked eye, but you get fed nonetheless. In flash, not only are the imperatives the same as in longer works, so are the tools.

Compression as a tiny pack of peanuts: All writing confronts dimension and perspective, but successful flash often plays with scale overtly, even exaggeratedly, by both expanding and compressing time, place, subject, you name it. To achieve compression, in particular—of urgency, voice, phrasing, image—try thinking of the short form as a diorama, a snow globe, a terrarium. Imagine a retired Navy pilot, at home, hunched over his treasured model airplanes, high on rubber cement and the magic of miniatures. Get crafty—with physics or a glue gun or whatever works. Fly inverted.

[PA crackles to life] "First Officer from the flight deck here. As we've now reached our cruising altitude, I'm handing the controls off to Captain Guisinger. Captain?"

Or are the peanuts a stand-in for the fact that your parents never loved you? Metaphor serves flash particularly well for its efficiency. For example, using the movements of a sloth to help us understand the slowness, ugliness, and determination of the author's grief at the core of the piece is why Jill Christman's "The Sloth" says as much as it does in 260 words. Using a dead moth on a windowsill as a stand-in for the entirety of the human experience is why Virginia Woolf can convey the entire human experience in 855 words in "The Death of a Moth."

Beginning Our Final Descent

A couple years ago, on a flight from Tampa to Boston, I experienced this thing called extreme turbulence for the first time, and it's amazing that I ever boarded a plane again. The plane bucked and jerked under our feet, and the wings yawed in and out of view through the weird little plane windows. I had time to think about all seven miles of gravity-soaked air between my feet and the ground. I was so certain we would die that my initial terror scooted over to make room for sadness: I wasn't ready for what I knew would be an abrupt, terrifying end. Ultimately, of course, the end looked like a safe touchdown on the tarmac at Logan, and it arrived slowly.

Descending seven miles in a commercial airliner is a stately process, imperceptible at times, and this was true even as we eased beneath bucking-bronco altitude. Our safe landing revealed itself slowly, like a piece of good news we were expecting, we just weren't sure when it would arrive. Commercial aircraft land on runways that stretch themselves out over a luxurious mile of gates, train-like luggage carts, and reflective, orange markers. In short, the flight was long with plenty of time to think and feel and project and brace ourselves, and the ending privileged itself with a leisurely unfolding. The metaphor I'm building here is obvious: that flight was a novel. Something Dickens wrote for which he was obviously paid by the word.

And now, some math! Fighter jets scoff at the seven miles above the earth where I sat weeping and sniveling between Boston and Tampa, and they don't need an entire mile to land and come to a stop. These flashy showoffs leave their contrails somewhere around 9.5 miles up, and the deck of an aircraft carrier is a mere quarter-mile of gleaming, laminated steel. And don't forget, while skidding off the runway at Logan might make a mess, that sort of error turns jets into submarines in the waters around the USS Flash Nonfiction.

Landing on a Short Runway

You're thinking, "This is all very nice, but what the hell does it mean when it's time for me to write an ending?" Let's take another look at Jericho Parms's flash essay, "Night."

She lands it like this:

> *The drapes, now hung high and wide, shield against the cold. In the same way, perhaps that*

> *dorm room back in Colorado still shelters stillness ... Even in the pitch-black night, this house remains a house, a camp where a boy or girl might hide, a tunnel where lovers might disappear, limbs tangled in the latitudes of design, until the rape of the world has passed, until we reach out and let the light back in.*

Notice how that last sentence mimics the structure of the whole piece by traveling through the house, the dorm room, the origins of the world, and the trauma of history; then it wraps it in the protective-but-soft-and-gentle curtain (that's the nod to the piece's own beginning) and sends the whole thing spinning toward the next beginning. The sentence employs echoes of the scenes, characters, and larger contextual elements of the piece, and not only that: it lands on this glimmering note of hope. That hope is like the arresting gear on the deck of the aircraft carrier: it hooks onto the undercarriage of the jet, bringing it from almost-light-speed to zero in less than a quarter-mile. Fighter pilots don't accidentally hook onto the arresting gear, by the way. It's a skill they develop over time. Parms makes it look easy here, but sticking a landing like that is worthy of a parade complete with ticker tape and a brass band.

Turning back to look at Daisy Hernandez's essay, "Wings," we can notice that the ending comprises the essay's last three sentences. We have known, since the first sentence's mention of the civil war, that this piece has a dark, dangerous core, but Hernandez has largely kept it offstage, kept us focused on the magic of raindrops with wings, the images of little girl hands and eyelashes, and the vaguely menacing violence of ripping wings off leafcutter ants as a game. The essay's descent begins when she deftly ties the Spanish word for wing (ala) to the word for soul (alma), drops in the phrase "boots of military men," and as the girls in the piece flee into the forest, the nose of the essay aims for the runway. She writes:

> *"From where she and her sister buried themselves for hours, she heard the screams of women and children as the soldiers plucked boys and girls from their homes, dragged the little ones through the mountains to enact the horrors we would one day read in newspapers: raping the children, throwing them onto trucks, into helicopters, into mass graves, and sometimes, yes sometimes, selling the children to childless couples, making infants and toddlers and older children, too, gifts from the mountains to military wives. Ala y Alma.*
>
> *"When the boots moved away, when the earth beneath them stopped its shivering, Maira and her baby sister would emerge from the forest, two girls in bare feet, waiting for the next storm."*

That final sentence, like the essay's opening sentence, is a multitasker. It moves the violence offstage, makes room for a short return to whatever passes for peace in this world, leaves us with an image of vulnerable, barefoot little girls, and spins us toward the next, inevitable attack. Please note that Hernandez chooses the phrase "baby sister" rather than just "sister" here at the end. Throughout, she uses them interchangeably, but the phrase "baby sister" emphasizes the vulnerability and the sweetness that coexist in the piece. And this word "storm" makes clear the ligature holding rain to ants to war.

Lastly, a look at the ending of Doyle's piece, "Two on Two." The mid-section of the piece is a 446-word sentence that whirls us around and around the airspace, sending us tumbling into this ending: " ... and I am happier than I have ever been, ever and ever, amen." Like most of the piece, there is nothing about this that should work. I mean, can you imagine the uproar in a workshop that "Once Upon A Time" would create? And by the ending, the piece has become so joyous as to almost become joy-porn, but it's by embracing and pushing further into that unabashedness, that I'm-in-love-and-I-don't-care-who-knows-it soaring, celebration of this otherwise simple scene that he makes it work. He's carefully and artfully aimed the piece at this ending with shameless phrases like "weeping, weeping, weeping" and "perfect, magic children." He erases any questions we might have had about what he's doing when he merges the last words with the ending of the Lord's Prayer. It's important to note that, if not for the genius use of basketball as both plot and metaphor, this piece would not have landed so much as it would have left flaming wreckage in place of the air control tower. In fact, it likely would never have left the ground at all.

Flight Swag: Some Tips, Tricks, and Lists to Take as You Disembark (Please Leave Unused Personal Flotation Devices and Vomit Bags Aboard the Aircraft)

Literary G-Forces: Think of the world of a flash piece as like that of a shoebox diorama—everything miniaturized and tactile, with perhaps imperfect scale, and some granular details that stick with you like craft glue.

Arrive and Depart on Time: If you quicken, heighten, or intensify the flash essay's stakes, voice, pacing, phrasing, imagery, meaning, and pulse (perhaps both in the writer and in the reader), you will create a sense of urgency and temporal scale suited to the vessel. How?

Lean on active verbs and precise nouns; keep syntax tight. Use pointed repetition of language and images. Pay attention to sound, both in the world of the piece and in the sentences on the page. Lean on precise sensory details.

Talk to the reader over the PA: Reflective Voice: sneak it in the way parents do with guilt or backhanded compliments.

Give metaphor the window seat: Metaphors are like your best travel buddy who lends you a packing cube so you can compress all your underwear into a tiny space in your suitcase. You can often communicate more efficiently by comparing a thing to another thing. Be nice to your metaphors: give them what they want.

Make it a round trip: If you can't figure out where to land, head back to where you started. Some good endings comprise a knowing nod at the beginning.

Look at the scenery: Study landscape paintings. If the painting is about a tree, the tree has a lot of detail. If the tree is in the background, it's made with a brushstroke or two. The background stuff is indicated more than it's drawn. Figure out what to indicate and what to draw.

Cross-training for cross-pollination: Read widely, from flash to memoir to essay collections to hybrid scholarship, and read outside of the genre, too: poetry, fiction, theory, drama, books about architecture or physics or intestinal disorders or polar exploration. Even the airline safety card.

*Items in this essay purporting to be aviation-related facts should not be taken as such. The authors are not pilots, aviation engineers, or physicists. They do not even like to fly. Alexis never did go to Space Camp, and Penny prefers sailing to flying. Any aviation information mentioned has been mined from search engines, terrifying television shows and movies, and from the authors' own shared flying fears and trauma bond.

17. REJECTION SUCKS AND THEN YOU DIE

MAYBE THE rejection letter was curt, churned out like a widget, or maybe it was wordy, with a misused semicolon, and penned in a respectable serif font. Maybe the missive employed grotesque let-you-down-easy phrasing such as, "There is much to admire about your work." (Imagine if some guy said this to you: "There is much to admire about your figure, but that face ... " The ignoramus sucks teeth and then licks lips. Or vice versa, as the ignoramus possesses no method for prioritizing offensive facial tics.)

Maybe the rejection was a personal email from the editor of the journal, and therefore lulled you into a false sense of comradeship—made you feel you were/are maybe, baby, on the cusp of the impenetrable circle jerk of the club. Now, now, be fair. The circle jerk dig comes from your stung inner bitch, lashing. (She's hurt.) "It's what comes after the 'but' that you have to listen for," Mom used to say. So, you listen for it. (It comes after the back-handed compliment but before the closing salutation.) In such always-a-bridesmaid letters, the journal is swimming in extraordinary work, or they just aren't into white girls right now, or they are looking specifically for third-person, non-linear chupacabras written in meter. (But definitely *no* sestinas. Who do you think you are, Bishop?) But ultimately, they sigh, they will have to (unfortunately) (regrettably) (sorry!) pass. (And just to have a little editorial fun at your pity party, you read the letter and tack the word "gas" onto this last line. They will have to pass *gas*.)

One rejection came in the mail on Crane's stationery with a woodblock print that just made you pine more keenly for membership. ("Please, sir," you imagined in your Pip voice, "just a glimpse of the roast duckling and roaring fire!") And as you (Pip) peered in, the people were radiant with cashmere sweaters and prep-school pedigrees, and real oak popped in the fireplace at the athenaeum. Okay, so you've seen too many movies. (But you knew some Exeter boys, and some are really like that. *Privileged* and over-medicated with underwhelming dicks you'd suck just to be on the inside for one lousy night in the back of someone's mom's Mercedes.)

Some rejections are just form letters, written with a bored affect in which you imagine the sender cutting and pasting a tight piece of coal into the body of the email, then yawning, then hitting send. And he's probably twenty-two, and that fact alone is grounds for (legal) (or clinical) indignation. You consider the havoc you could spend on his (probably) sexless, pathetic form. You could slice him into confetti, eat him for breakfast, mix so many metaphors that he wouldn't know what hit him, the little douche bag. You plot revenge, in which you appear in his office door in a fetching dress and say something like,

"Do you even know who I am?" You'll clutch your scorned manuscript and wave it under his pimply nose, "You'll pay for this, intern!" But still, SEND, and he has you withering.

In what job other than writing must you seek out frequent and concrete rejection? Okay, fine, but go get your own self-pitying rant. You have to seek it out if you want to get into the VIP mixer at AWP, even though you'll probably sulk in a corner, popping cheese balls, and trying to ignore the cob-webbed poet who just told you for the third time about his "new and selected." You have to suffer rejection's big blows, its mini-pelts, its hopes and just-maybes, and you have to shoulder into platitudes from non-writers and writers alike. Your mom: "Just keep at it, honey; you will get there. You're a great writer." (What does she know?) A well-published writer: "You have to get 100 rejections a year even to call yourself a writer." Fuck you. (Can you send me your submissions spreadsheet?) From other well-meaning types: "You'll get there; it takes time." (You are twenty-eight or thirty-seven or forty-six and have been writing seriously since nineteen. And you are good. You think. Pretty good. Maybe.)

The reason you write is that you want to be heard. And maybe you want to make money. Just a little, so you can stop fill-in-the-blank drudgery and spend more time writing and get better and get rejected less. Or get rejected better, or however that old Samuel Beckett line goes. And to be heard, you've got to publish in magazines, journals, and blogs. (Or wear a sandwich board on the highway, but this seems dangerous. And ineffective, as you live in Vermont.) You've simply got to get in the submission/rejection game.

So how do you handle it? They say that Fitzgerald was advised to drop Gatsby as a character, and Rudyard Kipling was told outright that he couldn't write. Gertrude Stein got a mocking rejection: "Hardly one copy would sell here. Hardly one. Hardly one." So, you figure there are a few options: you can be uber-rational and recognize that submitting is just a numbers game, but then you wouldn't be a writer. (You'd be an engineer. Or someone who is into *numbers.*) Option two: you can pretend to let it roll off (*fake it till you make it*) and preen yourself with your imaginary duck oil gland. Even though only a pose, it's useful because in your duck suit, you can do things you don't want to do—like email back the editor and say something along the lines of, "Thank you for your kind response. If you feel inclined or able, I would welcome any critical feedback you might have." (For this exercise you'll need an internet connection, a professional attitude, and a vomit bag.)

Or, you can do what I did today. You write back—polite, brief. You cry and think what a ridiculous baby you are but also how the rejection confirms some deep truth that you've been waiting for everyone else to discover. (Who are all these people? You don't know.) *You are a loser. A fraud.* So, you watch a little *Dateline* or *Air Disasters* and still feel crappy (see: daytime television) and think how writing/submitting is exactly like teenage dating. The indignity. The angst. The awkwardness and self-esteem so tenuously on parade. So you nap for an hour or two, crawling into a cocoon of yummy flannel with a non-threatening book, something by Nelson Demille, and you sleep it off. You sleep hard.

And when you wake, you sit down at the keyboard and use it all for fuel. The rejection emails, the slights you committed to memory like slam-book poetry, the anxiety, the yearning—you pour it all into the writing. You use it—even the petty, foul-mouthed stuff. (Maybe especially that stuff, the gooey innards of your own human frailty.) You use it all, for you are a writer. You put on your goddamned headgear and smile gawkily through your imaginary writer's braces. And you write. You fucking write.

18. BACK TO THE FUTURE: RETURNING WITHOUT THE ELIXIR

I HOPE YOU see by now that the elixir is there is no elixir. But there is magic in the making, and simple, effective plot elements can work, such as an ending that revolves back to the beginning again, without tying too neatly a bow around the dénouement.

This princess went on many quests, took many lashes across the bow, tasted the spray of the high seas, courted danger and derring-do, and ultimately, declined rescue. She was not a princess at all, in fact. She was just a girl, like me, with many bad ideas and good dreams who decided one day, and one after that, and again, to go for it—this writing life.

It was the year of Tropical Storm Irene when I declared that all of the writerly things would now be forthcoming, when I began to write more seriously, to publish a bit, and to apply for MFA programs. I had gotten the writer's conference bug, too, from the Atlanta one, so I decided to go for broke and attend the Writing Conference of

All Writing Conferences, AWP, which was being held in Chicago that year, the place of my birth. AWP stands for the Association of Writers and Writing Programs, and its annual conference, held in different American cities each year, draws numbers of attendees in the tens of thousands. No biggie.

Naturally, I lurched toward my first AWP with a hazy plan and a suitcase that weighed too much and cornered poorly. I had packed stilettos, cigarettes, scarves, and lipstick but forgotten my laptop, cotton swabs, and new business cards stamped with a retro typewriter logo. Forgetting cotton swabs on a trip is a bad omen indeed. My plan was breezy and vague: oh, I dunno—find some authentic deep-dish, go to a few panels, say smart things, be charming, and have literary types fall in love with me. If there's time, wrangle a book deal.

I've never been comfortable with networking-as-a-verb, but my skills in this area hadn't evolved since my twenties—awkwardness masked by flirtation. Incidentally, I gleaned this approach from an Anne Sexton biography that I read over ten years ago and interpreted not as a cautionary tale but as a primer on sex and dating.

I managed to get my AWP tote bag and lit swag, grab a slice served in a cardboard triangle, and check-in to my hotel room, all without incident. But it wasn't long after I had gotten to my room, scarfed the pie, and lined up my little sentry of toiletries by height, that I found myself overwhelmed and on the verge of panic. The conference hadn't even started, and this was not my usual existential panic but an actual can't-leave-the-room-and-function-in-public panic.

With nothing to do but strip down to my underpants and smoke in bed, I flipped through the ten-pound conference tome and tried to dam the tears with self-ridicule. I'll spare you most of the rest of my mega-conference meltdown, but I accomplished little and went home an exhausted rube. Unable to navigate logistics capably, I ended up in the wrong panel at least a half-dozen times (each in the wrong genre and with a title more obtuse than the last); told Sven Birkerts that his book, *The Art of Time in Memoir,* was "cool"; skulked around the book fair like a nervous woodland creature; collected business cards that would ultimately flounder in the bottom of my tote bag; and shouted "Hi!" to Cheryl Strayed in an elevator. (That's it—just "Hi!" followed by a pregnant ellipsis. I should've told her I loved her or thanked her for "writing like a motherfucker" ... something memorable.)

On the last night, I got invited—by way of the etiquette equivalent of the service elevator—to a VIP reception. Laureates, Pushcarts, NEA fellows, and National Book Award winners would be there: I was going to that room, the Gatsby room. Once there, however, I bored of the pomp and circumstance and sulked in a corner, popping cheesy poufs and getting hit on by a grandfatherly poet who mentioned his "new and selected" no fewer than eight times. The room was lovely, and Chicago too, but there was no elixir, and I was no princess to be saved.

I've learned so much since this first AWP, mainly that the "Write Like a Motherfucker" mugs sell out immediately, that the book fair and offsite parties are my jam, and that one week in a big city with eleven thousand other writer-nerds and a panel schedule that I am not qualified to read, administer, or ingest feels like a cross between entering the Matrix and setting myself on fire to my ADD-addled, possibly-pickled, aging brain.

Still, it's great fun. It's passably careerist—achievement unlocked! You can eat a lot of nachos and fried cheese in bed with your literary soul sister, and everyone is smart and cute and bespoke and bespectacled, and so talented, and so refreshingly fucked up. Even the famous ones and the almost-famous ones who are fucking themselves and each other or else they are writing about fucking themselves and each other. And you can smoke cigarettes like it's goddamned 1994, and someone is blasting Morrisey or A Tribe Called Quest and your navel is still impossibly snatched, and you're going to go outside and smoke deeply and heavily and meet a girl called Lorraine from Ohio who smokes cloves and is writing a graphic novel about her stepfather molesting her, and you're going to see a literary hero of yours, and your community friends, and your real writer friends who have read your shitty first drafts, and you will hate and love every minute of it.

Here are some other free tips.

HOW-TO-DO-AWP-IF-NOT-LIKE-A-GIRLBOSS-THEN-AT-LEAST-LIKE-SOMEONE-WHO-IS-NEITHER-A-CAPYBARA-NOR-AN-IMPOSTER

First, a pep talk. I come from a military family—my husband, brother-in-law, and father—all no-nonsense types. This can-do competency must live in my muscle memory, right? Early wakeups, hospital corners, overnight hiking trips in rugged New Hampshire mountains, extensive travel, and scrapping for respect in a big Catholic family: this was my childhood training. Dad was a recon Marine, for Christ's sakes; I can't get pummeled by a writers' conference.

Next, a plan and some rules of engagement. Instead of waiting until there, I grab my planner, the giant conference schedule booklet, and I highlight. I highlight like a motherfucker. I pick two panels per day and write them into my planner in tidy block print. Anything extra is gravy, but these two are non-negotiable. My schedule is set and reconnaissance complete.

The rules of engagement are simple: no side trips to City Park/Beach/Local Oddity; no hesitant lollygagging at the book fair (get in, get out—with solicitations and business cards); no window shopping on Expensive Shopping Street; no improvised chit-chat with famous writers; no panel reconnaissance on the fly, flipping through maps and schedules while bent over a subway grate; no sulking or crying; and no reading of panelist bios until safely extracted and home.

Packing List:

1. Combat Medic Kit.

If, like me, you suffer from both actual and imagined illnesses, you will want to be prepared in case of a blowout at the book fair, a paroxysm in panel, or (god forbid, crossing myself just in case) an embolism in flight. Make sure you pack the essentials: Vitamin C, pain reliever, prescriptions, antacids, calamine lotion, antiseptic, anti-diarrheals, anti-anxieties, anti-inflammatories, anti-psychotics, tourniquet, EpiPen, staple gun, and emergency flares (better safe than sorry). In case of emergency, you can find me, my kit, and my hypochondriac's diagnostic wheel at the *Brevity* table in the book fair. I'll be the one trying to fly a pinball machine.

2. Toiletries.

Red lipstick, moustache wax, pomade, cigarettes, mouthwash, flask, sunscreen, hair brush (?).

3. Snacks.

Leftover jellybeans and Peeps (which double as action figures for book fair dioramas), cigarettes (or nicotine gum), gum (nicotine gum), energy drinks, coffee (instant single-serve pouches are a lifesaver!), Emergen-C, Ziploc bags—for book fair loot and snacks you can pilfer from various hotel lobbies.

4. Old-Timey Typewriter*.

Who needs clothes? It's in a Warmer-than-Northeastern-or-Midwestern City this year, right?

*Check with local hipsters to see if this is still a thing.

5. Sandal/Mandal/Strappy Footwear.

You want to make your friends back in Michigan jealous of the tan lines on your feet.

6. Razor

To shave your toe tufts (see #5) or any other overgrown tufts in need of maintenance.

7. Extra tote bag.

A game of tote bag Red Rover could break out at any moment.

19. LAUNCHING YOUR BALLOON: ON PUBLICATION

NOT LONG before the Challenger Space Shuttle exploded at 48,000 feet over Florida and on the television screen squatted atop the A/V cart rolled into my fifth-grade classroom, my elementary school held a balloon launch: hundreds of balloon messages made lift off to points unknown, from a quiet, wooded knoll in southern New Hampshire. We wrote messages on scraps of paper—about what I can't remember—rolled them tightly, inserted the messages into the balloons, and passed them to Mr. Rube, my lanky fifth-grade teacher, who spent hours blowing them up.

Mr. Rube ran marathons, and he ran so much that he sometimes wore his running tights in class or we found him napping at his desk after lunch. I used to see him running through the neighborhood after school, and in that way that we project lives of great mystery onto our teachers, I imagined that even overnight Mr. Rube dashed through the sleepy streets of our city, and that's what made him so tired.

After lunch on the day of the balloon launch, we found Mr. Rube at his desk, beaming from behind a curtain of shiny red orbs that danced and bounced all around him. I understood then that we were engaged in a magical transaction—from our own pens, from our little classroom, to the balloons, to the sky, to the world. Whether the messages shot to heaven or snagged on a tree or sagged sadly to Earth or burned up upon re-entry was now up to the universe.

Some months later, after the Challenger exploded and after Christa McAuliffe, the beloved schoolteacher from nearby Concord, died in the explosion, I got a reply to my balloon message from Virginia. Virginia! I couldn't believe it. I looked it up on the map and traced my finger the 600-odd miles my balloon had traveled. I couldn't remember then what I had written, but I hoped that it was important. I hoped that I had said something worthy of such a journey. I remember feeling sad, too, knowing that Christa McAuliffe's message would never be delivered, wondering what her balloon might have said.

Here I launch my second book—a memoir of craft and love and labor—and I find myself overcome by the same glee and awe I felt in the early winter of 1986 as I watched hundreds of red balloons twirl off into the gray New Hampshire sky. I'm no stranger to breathing life into sentences and then sending them into the world, but breathing life into a book and then sending it into the world is different; it's not only the scale of the project but also the implicit request one makes of the reader for their sustained attention. These words now belong to the world. I hope mainly that I've said something important, something worthy of the miles they travel to reach you.

APPENDIX A: PROMPT-DITTIES

4. *The Hero Embarks on a Quest* prompt

In this essay, the title is a nod to Joseph Campbell's monomyth, the hero's journey, which is a mythic structure Campbell outlined as a way of storytelling—a way of understanding and rendering experience. The myth comprises twelve steps in three acts in which the "hero" (protagonist, narrator, speaker, character, and so forth, depending on the genre and form) is transformed. In Act One, the hero leaves their "ordinary world" for an adventure or challenge calling them to the "special world." In Act Two, the special world, the hero faces small and large defeats, wrestles with some central conflict, and then really wrestles with said conflict. At the climax in Act Two, the hero overcomes or resolves said conflict in some way that has changed them; they have prevailed, but not always in the way one expects. The hero returns home, to the ordinary world, in Act Three, with the elixir—some newfound insight or skill or object—that they will now share with those back home. The myth is popular with narrative writers of all stripes, including screenwriters, novelists, graphic novelists, memoirists, and so forth, so there are tons of resources both on and offline about how to use it in writing and developing story. One of my favorite adaptations of the mythic structure appears in Christopher Vogler's, *The Writer's Journey*; in it, Vogler posits seventeen steps in three acts, and I've seen all manner of permutations. The point is not to use the hero's journey strictly as a template, though that might work if you're sketching out early plot or character arcs. In my case, I used the writing conference as the call to action, the meeting "boy writer" as both an introduction of the central conflict and as a meeting of allies; the ordeal was the transgression; and the elixir was, well, complicated.

For this prompt, I challenge you to write a short narrative (perhaps a short story, a personal essay, or a flash essay or story) using some aspect of Campbell's monomyth as a central structural element or elements—be as loose or prescriptive as is comfortable. Perhaps there's a fictional or personal story you want or have been trying to tell whose skeleton sags; try propping it up with a "call to adventure" in the right place; try fleshing out the "ordeal"; try rendering an "inmost cave" moment for your hero; figure out what the elixir is or isn't.

11. *New Fish* prompt

This essay took me so long to write that my essayist card was nearly revoked. My struggle writing it initially, and forever after that, was that I kept pulling the reader aside to say how much I was learning, how much I had learned, but there was no set design or ambient light or smells or characters with moveable limbs or other sentient beings or any feet on the ground. And then I stumbled on the phrase, *I have people*, while revising one day, and I said, that's it! *That's* what I've come to say. So I burned the old versions and wrote a new one all in scene, and I found a place toward the end to drop "I have people." Now I had the shape and spine of the essay, so I went back in and stitched minimal reflective material, like one fine thread that weaves through an otherwise (I hope) cinematic experience. This made it so I had to say the thing I had come to say only once, and with brio.

For this prompt, choose a story (whether personal or fictional) where the hero is shaken up by entering an especially "special" world. These could be traumas or travels or any dramatically dislocating experiences. Write the thing mostly or only in scene at first. Let the jarring vicissitudes have center stage while you quietly work to the one (or two) important but subtle (maybe even quiet) insights. Let the experience loom large and loud, try to make the hero small—or growing ever-smaller, and whisper the insight(s).

14. *Lilacs in the Dooryard* prompt

"The conflict between the will to deny horrible events and the will to proclaim them aloud is the central dialectic of psychological trauma."

Judith Lewis Herman, Trauma and Recovery

Many traumatized people expose themselves, seemingly compulsively, to situations reminiscent of the original trauma; this tendency can help or hurt the writer (or person) depending on what they do with it. Freud thought the aim of repetition was to gain mastery, but new clinical research shows mastery is a myth. Rather, repetition causes further suffering for the victims or for people in their surroundings. Obviously, I wish to move into a better state where I'm not always having intrusive thoughts about my rapes or other traumas, but in this essay, I became interested in using that repetitive tendency as a scaffolding for circling round and round obsession.

Traumatic events can be obvious material for the creative nonfiction writer, but since such narratives are ubiquitous, the essayist or memoirist might keep in mind certain principles and strategies to create a fresh take on trauma and to avoid writing that is merely therapeutic, rather than artistic. Craft challenges posed by trauma narrative often require special care to keep them firmly in the lane of art, rather than therapy or catharsis.

In the case of this essay, I leaned into the repetitive suffering (counterintuitively, I suppose) as a way of assaying deeper and deeper into these complex and overwhelming experiences, and then I used research as a way of lifting those rendered experiences, I hope, to somewhere beyond the merely or strictly personal.

The very nature of trauma lends itself to non-linear storytelling and experimental forms (for example, lyric essays, hermit crab essays, collage, and multi-media forms), so I allowed the story to come in waves and cross currents. Research shows that trauma fractures memory and one's sense of chronology, so the creative nonfiction writer can use this sense of fracture as architecture for the writing rather than fighting to fit the narrative into a linear timeline. Whether writing about jail, addiction, cancer, or car crashes, the memoirist/essayist can take their cue from neuroscience and render the story non-linearly. In fact, such a rendering might make the piece not only truer, but also better.

In addition to craft, and despite one's desire to avoid merely therapeutic writing, the trauma writer does face significant personal, emotional, and psychological peril by confronting such material. To write it well, one must dwell in the experience and return to the scene of the trauma, an act that can create a kind of emotional hangover. Managing such efforts is difficult and takes time, so if you do wish to pursue a trauma narrative with these thoughts or the following prompt in mind, I urge you to work slowly, to work kindly with yourself, and to ask for help early and often—with both the writing and the subject.

For this prompt, write a story—whether personal, fictional, or allegorical—that is fraught with trauma or some of the heavier burdens of the human condition. Rather than attempting to write it neatly or linearly, write its larger strokes by using its own logic, by leaning into the intuition of the experience itself: write it out of order, or in burrowing rings, or in some strange pattern that makes sense to you. An architecture organic to the weight and shape of the thing will emerge. And then do some research on the subject, which you can then weave in to add resonance and texture for a wider readership.

SHOUTOUTS FROM THE RUNWAY: RESOURCES, REFERENCES, AND EPHEMERA

Preface

Rappaport, Stephen. "Dragging the Bottom for Scallops." *The Ellsworth American*, 18 March 2015.

Vonnegut, Kurt. "The Shapes of Stories" (lecture). *Ted.* https://ed.ted.com/best_of_web/ZG7Q2obA

Williams, Allison. "A Brief Guide to Essays." *Brevity*, 1 August 2017. https://brevity.wordpress.com/2017/08/01/a-brief-guide-to-essays/

1. A Portrait of the Writer as a Young Obsessive-Compulsive

"Bell Biv Devoe Chart History." *Billboard.* https://www.billboard.com/music/bell-biv-devoe/chart-history/BSI

Ewan, Rebecca Fish. "Doodling Hippocamp: 2017." *Brevity*, 16 September 2017. https://brevity.wordpress.com/2017/09/16/writers-conferences-doodling-hippocamp-2017/

Kidder, Tracy. "On His Early Education in Writing." *New York State Writers Institute*, 2004. https://www.youtube.com/watch?v=QJX4Iri0zA4

2. Those Who Can, Teach

Dillard, Annie. *The Writing Life*. New York: Harper Collins, 1989. Print

3. Paper Girl

"Robert Wallack." *Daily News Obituaries*, 15 Jan. 2014. https://obituaries.newburyportnews.com/obituary/robert-wallack-772718871

4. The Hero Embarks on a Quest: Girl Writer Meets Boy Writer

Gilbert, Jack. *The Great Fires: Poems 1982-1992*. New York: Knopf, 2000. Print

Jarman, Mark. "Ground Swell." *Poets.org*. Academy of American Poets. 1 Feb. 2008. Web. 27Mar. 2012. <http://www.poets.org/viewmedia.php/prmMID/15642>.

Krakauer, Jon. *Into the Wild*. New York: Anchor Books, 1997. Print

5. But Then You Read

Baldwin, James. “The Doom and Glory of Knowing Who You Are.” *Life Magazine*, 24 May 1963. Print

6. Beware the Writer; Writer, Beware

Didion, Joan. *Slouching Towards Bethlehem*. New York: Farrar, Straus, and Giroux, 1968. Print

7. Ars Poetica

Baldwin, James. *The Fire Next Time*. New York: Dial Press, 1963. Print

Gornick, Vivian. *The Situation and the Story: The Art of Personal Narrative.* New York: Farrar, Straus, and Giroux, 2001. Print

Marquart, Debra. https://debramarquart.com/

Vogler, Christopher. *The Writer's Journey: Mythic Structure for Writers.* Studio City, CA: Michael Wiese Productions, 2007. Print

Pate, Alexs. https://innocentclassroom.com/our-company/alexs-pate/

Field, Syd. *Screenplay: The Foundations of Screenwriting.* New York: Bantam Dell, 1984. Print

Davis, Angela. *Are Prisons Obsolete?* New York: Seven Stories Press, 2003. Ebook

Baca, Jimmy Santiago. *A Place to Stand.* New York: Grove Atlantic, 2001. Print

Alexander, Michelle. *The New Jim Crow: Mass Incarceration in the Age of Colorblindness.* New York: The New Press, 2012. Print

Morrison, Toni. *Playing in the Dark: Whiteness and the Literary Imagination.* New York: Vintage Books, 1992. Print

8. Remembering the Cockroaches: On Doubt in Creative Nonfiction

Berger, John. *Keeping a Rendezvous.* Vintage, 2011. Print

Deveare Smith, Anna. "In Conversation With, David Rubenstein Lecture," 2019. https://www.youtube.com/watch?v=R8orTcppRvg

9. On Race, Identity, and Narrative Craft: An Interview with David Mura by the Author

Mura, David. *Turning Japanese: Memoirs of a Sansei.* New York: Double Day, 1991. Print

Mura, David. *A Stranger's Journey: Race, Identity, and Narrative Craft in Writing.* University of Georgia Press, 2018. Print

Mura, David. http://www.davidmura.com/

10. White Writers' Tears: An Open Letter to White Accomplices in the (Specifically American) Literary Community

Rankine, Claudia. http://claudiarankine.com/

Palmares Meadows, Jen. https://jenpalmaresmeadows.com/

Johnston, Amanda. https://www.amandajohnston.com/

VIDA. https://www.vidaweb.org/the-count/

12. How About This for Meta?

Fischer, Michael. https://www.ilhumanities.org/michael-fischer/

13. Digging for Mud Bugs and Story Bones

Hurd, Barbara. *Listening to the Savage: River Notes and Half-Heard Melodies.* University of Georgia Press, 2016. Print

14. Lilacs in the Door Yard

"97 of Every 100 Rapists Receive No Punishment, RAINN Analysis Shows." RAINN, Rape, Abuse, and Incest National Network. http://rainn.org/news- room/97-of-every-100-rapists-receive-no-punishment.html

Hopper, James and David Lisak, "Why Rape and Trauma Survivors Have Fragmented and Incomplete Memories," *Time,* December 9, 2014. http://time.com/3625414/rape-trauma-brain-memory.html

15. Writing is Hard, and It Takes a Long Time

Conley, Susan. https://www.susanconley.com/

16. Traveling Companions & Flying Pinball Machines: How to Launch and Land Your Flash CNF

Guisinger, Penny https://pennyguisinger.com/

Editors of Hippocampus Magazine. *Getting to the Truth: The Craft and Practice of Creative Nonfiction.* Lancaster, PA: Hippocampus Books, 2021

18. Back to the Future: Returning Without the Elixir

Birkerts, Sven. *The Art of Time in Memoir.* Graywolf, 2008. Print

The Rumpus "Write Like a Motherfucker" mug https://store.therumpus.net/product/write-like-a-mother-fucker-coffee-mug/

Strayed, Cheryl. https://www.cherylstrayed.com/

ACKNOWLEDGMENTS

Some of these essays, in some form or another, first appeared in other publications.

"A Portrait of the Writer as a Young Obsessive-Compulsive" first appeared on the *Brevity* Blog (April 2014).

A version of "The Hero Embarks on a Quest: Girl Writer Meets Boy Writer" first appeared as the essay, "The Geography of Consolation," which won the New Millennium Writings Nonfiction Prize in 2013 and was published in the *New Millennium Writings* 2014 anthology.

"But Then You Read" appeared in a much different form as part of a longer books review, "Marrying the Personal and Political," in *Fourth Genre* (Fall 2016).

"Beware the Writer; Writer, Beware" was first published on *Brevity* as the essay, "On Didion and the 'Selling Out' Mantra" (June 2012).

"Remembering the Cockroaches" first appeared in *Passages North's* "Writers on Writing Series" (September 2014).

"On Race, Identity, and Narrative Craft: An Interview with David Mura" first appeared on *Brevity* (December 2018).

"White Writers' Tears" appeared as "An Open Letter to White Allies in the Literary Community" on *Jaded Ibis Press* (June 2016).

"New Fish" was first published as the essay, "The Right to Remain," in *The Rumpus* in 2015 and named a Best American Essays Notable in 2016.

A version of "Digging for Mudbugs and Story Bones" appeared on *Brevity* in a book review of Barbara Hurd's *Listening to the Savage* (November 2016).

"Lilacs in the Dooryard" first appeared as the essay, "Common Purple Lilac," in the 2017 Mercer University Press anthology, *A Second Blooming*, edited by Susan Cushman. The essay subsequently appeared on *Full Grown People* in June 2017 and was listed as a BAE Notable in 2018.

"Traveling Companions and Flying Pinball Machines ... ," co-written by this author and also-a-Vine-Leaves-Press author, Penny Guisinger, first appeared as the essay, "Takeoffs and Landings: How to Launch and Land Your Flash CNF," in the 2021 Books by Hippocampus anthology, *Getting to the Truth: The Craft and Practice of Creative Nonfiction*, edited by Rae Pagliarulo and Donna Talarico

"Rejection Sucks and Then You Die" first appeared in *The Rumpus* (April 2013).

A version of "Back to the Future: Returning Without the Elixir" first appeared on the *Brevity* Blog as the essay, "The Ultimate Guide to Not Letting the AWP Do You" (March 2013).

Big, bravocado claps of gratitude go to Melanie Faith, my kind, generous, and encouraging editor at Vine Leaves Press for this book. I couldn't have done it without you.

Thanks so very much to Amie McCracken and Jessica Bell and the Vine Leaves Press team who continue to champion good work and to do so tirelessly and with good humor.

Thanks to Mom for gifting me a special writing retreat in a special place.

Thanks to David Mura for his friendship and for allowing our interview to have a second life here.

Thanks to Penny Guisinger for contributing her work to this book, but more so for her ongoing contributions of friendship. She is now an Iron Pyrite Star member.

Thanks to Suzanne Strempek-Shea for being there and listening and guiding so kindly, so fully.

Thanks to Rae Pagliarulo and Donna Talarico, the editors of Books by Hippocampus, for allowing me to reprint the essay so soon after the publication of their first amazing anthology. And I thank them, doubly, for their early endorsement of this book.

Melanie Brooks read and blurbed the book first, and I am grateful for her friendship, colleagueship, and her heartfelt endorsement.

Thanks to Sarah Einstein for being another early, clutch reader and thoughtful endorser of the book.

Thanks to Tim Hillegonds for his early, generous read, and for his all-around good literary citizenship.

Thanks to Michael Fischer for allowing our conversation to take flight.

Thanks to Dawn Carleton for taking a flyer on me, and for her mentorship.

Thanks to Mary Findley for passing the Nerds and laughs at all of the meetings.

Thanks to Jeff Higgins for finding a way.

Thanks to Dinty Moore for his support.

Last but not least, thank you to Lauren and Hannah—who helped me survive a pandemic and a book.

VINE LEAVES PRESS

CPSIA information can be obtained
at www.ICGtesting.com
Printed in the USA
LVHW041930230122
709144LV00009B/886

9 781925 965766